best sex writing
2006

best sex writing 2006

Edited by
Felice Newman and
Frédérique Delacoste

CLEIS PRESS

Published in the United States by Cleis Press Inc.,
P.O. Box 14697, San Francisco, California 94114.

Printed in the United States.
Cover design: Scott Idleman
Cover photograph: Marin/Getty
Text design: Frank Wiedemann
Logo art: Juana Alicia
First Edition.
10 9 8 7 6 5 4 3 2 1

Library of Congress Cataloging-in-Publication Data

Best sex writing 2006 / edited by Felice Newman and Frédérique Delacoste.
    p. cm.
ISBN 1-57344-237-2 (pbk. : alk. paper)
1. Sex—United States. I. Newman, Felice. II. Delacoste, Frédérique.
HQ18.U5B45 2006
306.70973—dc22
                              2006006516

Acknowledgments

The editors are grateful to our authors, and to Scott Idleman, Karen Quigg, Regina Marler, Gary Morris, Mark Rhynsburger, Kim Wylie, Elise Cannon, Kevin Votel, Luke Carmody, Rich Freese, and in particular to Diane Levinson and Chris Fox for helping Cleis Press remain as independent and iconoclastic as ever.

This book is for Constance and Melanie.

CONTENTS

Introduction

This was the year that the U.S. Attorney General's office declared war on porn once again. In an action that reminds one of the Meese Commission of the 1980s, we have the current AG tilting at the windmills of human desire. The new federal mandate calls for clamping down on Internet porn, and they are targeting hard-core BDSM and fetish sites, specifically the sites least likely to raise the sympathy of most Americans.

Will the campaign against depictions of fantasy sadism and depravity at home make us forget the images of real-life sadism and depravity at Abu Ghraib? The irony would be comic if it weren't so tragic.

Representations of sexuality are ubiquitous, as anyone who has ever clicked a mouse can attest. Yet even in the relative democracy of the Internet, personal revelations about sex are often cheesy, or coated with a layer of false sophistication.

Despite our overexposed culture (or perhaps because of it), we forget how courageous it is to write authentically about sex. We aren't used to honest depictions of sex. What we've been given is airbrushed, or if not airbrushed, then at least contrived in its imitation of the raw physical expression of emotion. So idealized is the sexuality we've been taught to live up to that the real experience may leave us feeling embarrassed or shameful. Real sex is not necessarily pretty. Cataclysmically erotic experiences don't necessarily leave you feeling Downy Fresh. Even in the realm of Hearts and Flowers, all is not hearts and flowers.

Thankfully, sexual inventiveness has not been worn down by excessive disclosure. Innocent beginnings, with all their implied freedom and spontaneity, are still possible. True love *is* real, generosity of spirit abounds, and good politics win out. Integrity, self-knowledge, and the ecstasy of transcending the self to touch the Universal—all are to be found within these pages.

Taken together, the essays in *Best Sex Writing 2006* comprise a detailed, direct survey of the contemporary American sexual landscape, one that we at Cleis Press have helped to shape over the past quarter century.

The authors in *Best Sex Writing 2006* write movingly—and authentically—about sexual politics, sexual culture, and sexual expression. They offer an in-depth look at sex the way it actually happens in America today. Their work is humorous, informative, challenging, sexy, serious, deeply disturbing, both thoughtful and thought-provoking.

Here then is the fruit of their labors, both in the reporting and in the reality.

Felice Newman
March 2006
San Francisco

Where's the Sin? An Anti-Sermon
Shalom Auslander

Yesterday afternoon I received an e-mail containing the names and addresses of hundreds of horny MILFs right in my neighborhood, which I deleted without reading. I didn't even bother opening the one about a gorgeous teen taking it deep in her ass, and when, curious, I opened an e-mail titled "Looking to Refinance?" a new window popped up on my desktop featuring an animated picture of an attractive blonde girl with an enormous black dildo thrusting in and out of her mouth. I rolled my eyes, clicked the mouse impatiently to close the window, and sighed to myself, "Oh, come on, already."

What's happening to me?

I wake up in the morning to the sounds of a lesbian in Howard Stern's studio; blindfolded, she is trying to guess which of three contestants is her girlfriend by licking their pussies. I yawn, switch from FM to AM, and try to find the weather report.

I trudge through Manhattan, oblivious to the towering billboards of near-naked models, oblivious, too, to the near-naked women around me. Two girls hurry by; their asses read "Juicy." How come, I wonder, you can never get a goddamn cab in this city?

I arrive home in the evening, turn on the television, and I'm met with the latest music video from the latest teenage ingenue, bent over, her barely covered ass shaking at the camera. I reach for the remote and change the channel. "There's never anything on," I sigh.

What the *hell* is happening to me?

Genesis 2:25—*The man and his wife were both naked and they felt no shame.*

Genesis 3:6–7—*When the woman saw that the fruit of the tree was good for food and pleasing to the eye, and also desirable for gaining wisdom, she took some and ate it; she also gave some to her husband, who ate it. Then the eyes of both of them were opened and they realized they were naked.*

The great eleventh-century French Torah commentator Rashi asks, "What does it mean that they realized they were naked? Even a blind man knows that he is naked." Rashi goes on to explain that having eaten from the Tree of Knowledge, Adam and Eve suddenly knew of good and of evil, of morality and of immorality, of sin and of virtue, and they were ashamed.

Genesis 3:11—God busts them.

Genesis 3:14—God curses them.

Genesis 3:24—God chases them from Eden and bars the Gates of Paradise so that they may never return.

And what's the first thing they do? What is the very first thing that they do?

Genesis 4:1—And Adam knew Eve.

They fucked.

The very next chapter. The very first verse. *And Adam knew Eve.*
The very. First. Verse.

Pre sin, not a single mention of fucking (aside from the somewhat clinical reference in Chapter Two to a man and woman "becoming one flesh"). Rashi doesn't mention this, but it's right there in the text: sin comes along, Adam and Eve get chased out of Paradise by a bellicose Deity, they are cursed for generations with toil and agonizing labor, the gate to their former home is blocked for eternity by two belligerent Cherubim and something called the Blade of the Turning Sword, and what do they do?

They fuck.

And Adam knew Eve.

No setting up their apartment, no stopping at Ikea for funky lighting, no sin offerings to their Lord, no journeying to Ur, or to Goshen, or to The Land Which I Will Show You.

The moment they knew sin, they fucked.

I know how they felt.

I spent most of the first eighteen years of my life in all-male yeshivas (same thing as madrassas, only with a different book), being instructed in the wily ways of the Evil Inclination, the dangerous lure of women and of the horrible punishments for wasting seed. In the Yeshiva of Spring Valley, the girls were safely hidden away in a separate building that stood across a busy four-lane thoroughfare. At summer camp the girls had their own campus, half a mile away from the boys, through a forbidding, densely wooded forest guarded by watchful camp rabbis and religious camp counselors. Even the bus that traveled from my Orthodox town into Manhattan had separate seating—men sat on the right, women on the left, and a thick woolen curtain hung down between them.

I was never hornier.

If they forbade me to look at it, I wanted to touch it. If they forbad me to touch it, I wanted to lick it. If they forbade me to lick it, I wanted to shave it, pierce it, and put things inside it.

When the rest of my fourth-grade Torah class had moved on to the story of Abraham, I was still picturing the orgies back in Sodom. When Rabbi Glatzer read the verse "And Abraham knew Sarah," I pictured my busty matriarch in fishnets and high heels, with a cumshot across her face.

"Yeah, that's it, Abraham," I thought, "know her. Know the fucking shit out of her."

Purgatory was no deterrent. If I burned for it, I yearned for it.

And Adam knew Eve.

Like Adam and Eve, once I learned of sin, there was no going back. If they'd really wanted to cool me down, they'd have told me everything was permissible. Permissibility is a cold shower.

I need sin.

I need transgression.

I need to violate, to desecrate, to abominate.

And so today, whether it's lesbians on Howard Stern or Britney's new boobs or horny MILFs in my neighborhood, whether it's the radio or the television or the Internet, I yawn, and I reach for the dial, or the remote, or the mouse pad, and I find myself wondering: Where's the sin?

It's all so...allowed.

Where's the violation? The desecration? The abomination? Please, take me back in time—take me back and book me the Presidential Suite in the Gomorrah Hilton with Lot, all his daughters, a ten-pack of nipple clamps, and a gallon of Wet Lube.

There was a time when the exposed nipple of a national sex symbol would have generated something more than derision. But what's a nipple anymore? If I check my e-mail in the morning, I can see a dozen nipples before breakfast. If Janet Jackson wants to be naughty, provocative, sexual—if she hopes in some way to even pretend to be transgressive—she and her choreographers are going to have to figure out a way for Justin Timberlake to "accidentally" fist her asshole while she "inadvertently" eats out her sister.

Where's the sin?

Fuck saving trees. Fuck whales and lemurs and spotted owls. Save sin. Save sex. Save fucking.

Save thongs.

What a thrill that used to be!—that stolen glimpse of a woman's panties as she bent over in the gym, or the restaurant, or the supermarket, the frenzied hope as I circled back around the canned goods aisle that she would still be there, squatting down to get a bag of sugar. Now I can't get away from the damn things. Where's the sin? I've gone from glimpsing a woman's thong and thinking about how much I'd like to tear those pants off and fuck her, to thinking about how much I wish she'd just pull her fucking pants up.

Thongs are dead for me.

Thongs are dead for me, and TV and advertising and the Internet and Howard Stern and J.Lo killed them. What's next, J.Lo? Vaginas? Will that be a trend? Women just walking around with their vaginas sticking out because J.Lo did that on her last video? Are you going to ruin vagina for me next?

I want my sin back. I want transgression.

Iniquity.

Abominations.

So here is where I find myself—a religiously irreligious, devoutly nondevout, strictly nonkosher former religious student—in a sexual position more strange than anything dreamt of on the Internet: silently cheering for the self-appointed, holy-spirit-anointed morality police, for the podium-pounding religious right, for the outraged moral majority, for Bill O'Reilly and Sean Hannity, for the Mothers Against Everything, for the fist wavers with their balsa-wood crucifixes and their typo-laden placards shouting about The Children, for the pandering pornography-policy-passing politicians, for the bills restricting online porn and strip clubs and prostitution, for the fire-and-brimstone LA County Sheriffs kicking in the doors of porno production companies.

Lock it up, boys. Shut it down.

Burn it, ban it, bury it in the vaults beneath the vaults beneath the Vatican and seal it with the sign of the Seven Seals.

I'm getting hot just thinking about it.

SMARTLY WRITTEN ESSAY IN THE SLOW DECLINE OF SEXUAL MYSTICISM

The Coming Boom
Annalee Newitz

I'm in Newark, New Jersey, in a small room dominated by a large conference table. There are no windows, and no sounds except for the whir of the ventilation system. "This is going to be great," my host, Rutgers neuropsychologist Barry Komisaruk, says, grinning.

A woman walks in with a large black duffel bag and shuts the door. "This is my graduate student Janice Breen," Komisaruk says. Breen opens the bag, unpacks a few electromechanical components, and begins to assemble them using a screwdriver.

"So what do you call this?" I ask. The device looks like a tampon attached to a hefty electric toothbrush, which is in turn wired to a box with a glowing red digital readout.

"It's the, um, contraption," Breen answers distractedly, hunting for an outlet.

"Actually, it's called the calibrated vaginal stimulator," Komisaruk tells me. "It's a modified tampon attached to a transducer for measuring the force that women apply to the vaginal wall."

The tampon looks big enough to be in the supersize range and is connected at a forty-five-degree angle to the metal handle, which houses the transducer. Scores of women have inserted Breen's contraption into their vaginas. (The tampons are disposed of after each use.) As I fiddle with the tampon, the pressure from my fingers registers as a few grams of force.

"Women self-stimulate," Komisaruk explains, "and we use fMRIs"—functional magnetic resonance imaging—"to look at which parts of their brains respond."

I stare at the instrument in my hands.

"Basically," Komisaruk concludes, "it's a dildo."

The tools are crude, but that's because the science of sexual arousal is still young. Viagra revolutionized the field in the 1990s. The little blue pill that gets blood flowing to the right places at that special moment became a blockbuster for Pfizer, spawning Eli Lilly's Cialis and GlaxoSmithKline's Levitra. Millions now take these drugs to kick-start an evening of private recreation.

Flush with success in the fight against "erectile dysfunction," the pharmaceutical industry set out to develop Viagra for women. First, researchers simply gave women the same pill that worked so well for men. The good news: The drug does pump a woman's genitals full of blood. But it won't necessarily get her frisky.

The results were surprising and frustrating to the pharmaceutical industry, which had assumed that what was good for the gander would be good for the goose. Julia Heiman, a psychology professor and director of the Kinsey Institute, conducted some of Pfizer's Viagra studies and found that while some women "really noticed their genitals" and felt aroused, others "barely paid attention" to them and weren't aroused at all. In other words, signals originating from these women's genitals just weren't translating into conscious desires. That insight put a new target in researchers' sights: the female brain itself. "The brain is where things are made sexual," Heiman explains. "It's the organ that causes us to be attracted to certain body types or looks. That kind of preference isn't processed in the genitals."

Even before Pfizer abandoned the bottom-up approach in 2004, the industry began investigating top-down options. The reigning wisdom these days is that making arousal drugs for women will involve targeting the female brain the way Viagra targets the male vascular system.

The first arousal drugs aimed at women's gray matter are expected to be on the market in the next couple of years. The active ingredient: testosterone, a "male" hormone that is also naturally present in women's bodies in smaller quantities. Procter & Gamble plans to release a testosterone patch, Intrinsa, and Illinois-based BioSante is entering Phase III clinical trials with its testosterone formulation, LibiGel. Even so, most researchers agree that testosterone isn't the end of the story. Testosterone drugs will never have a direct, rapid effect on women the way Viagra does on men, because it's a hormone that fosters an overall sense of strength and well-being rather than specifically catalyzing sexual arousal. More promising is a drug called PT-141, which is being developed by Palatin Technologies in New Jersey. The first in a new class of drugs called melanocortin agonists, PT-141 targets the central nervous system. Early trials show both genital arousal and increased sexual desire in women who take it. But even more precisely targeted drugs are coming—those that won't light up the entire nervous system in the blind hope of hitting pleasure buttons, but actually home in on parts of the brain that are directly connected to arousal and orgasm.

The total market for male arousal drugs is $2.7 billion per year and rising. Thanks to a study published in the *Journal of the American Medical Association* estimating that 43 percent of women are dissatisfied with sex—as opposed to 31 percent of men—the market for a pink Viagra could be even bigger. For now, those future billions are locked up in the labs where scientists are attempting to reverse engineer the female orgasm.

Ken Maravilla is small, dignified, and quiet. He comes across as someone who would never tell a dirty joke, which is why he's perfectly cast in his role as one of the few radiologists in the United States to specialize in examining the brain scans of sexually aroused women. But there's nothing prurient here—he's in it only for the magnet.

Nobody in the lab calls it the fMRI machine, and certainly nobody bothers to say "functional magnetic resonance imaging." It's just "the magnet." And the part of the room-sized machine that seeks out oxygen differentials in your blood—that's called the doughnut.

Maravilla's tiny office is in the basement at the University of Washington in Seattle, behind two large metal doors emblazoned with the warning: *Danger—restricted access—strong magnetic field—the magnet is always on!* Working with the Kinsey Institute's Heiman and other psychologists, Maravilla has been monitoring what happens to women's brains when they watch what he calls "visual material."

Heiman is less delicate. "They're erotic videos," she says. "Female-friendly films by Candida Royale."

The point of the experiment is to understand what happens to the female brain during arousal. "A lot of people thought there would be a single sex center in the brain, but that isn't the case," Maravilla says. "In fact, multiple areas are activated."

Women wear video goggles in the magnet so they can see the

movies. They watch five minutes of Candida Royale, then five minutes of a flick about mitochondria. Then the process is repeated: five minutes of arousal, five minutes of edutainment. Over a period of roughly half an hour, Maravilla examines what the difference is between a brain on Candida and a brain on Nova.

So can female arousal be quantified? The answer, Maravilla's team concludes, is yes. Brains in the throes of excitement light up in consistent, measurable ways. Furthermore, it turns out that excited women's brains look almost exactly like excited men's brains. Maravilla boots up his laptop and shows me several MR images of brains whose glowing hypothalamuses and cingulate cortices are neural maps of female desire. Then he takes me down a short hall and ushers me into the fMRI's tiny control booth, where I meet Seth Friedman, a researcher and colleague of Maravilla's. We chat about how difficult it is to study cognitive and genital arousal with MRI alone. "They're two parallel responses separated by a couple of feet," Friedman says. Either you stick someone's head in the magnet, or you stick their privates in—but you can't do both at once.

"You'd really need a double doughnut to do it right," Maravilla says wistfully. Friedman laughs, and then Maravilla cracks a smile, the first I've seen on his face all day.

Getting good images of the aroused female brain is easy. It's orgasm that's the problem. In the doughnut, the slightest head movement ruins the scan. Even if a test subject holds her head perfectly still while masturbating, the parts of the brain responsible for motor control are switched on, muddying the picture. "You'll see vaginal sensory input to the brain," Komisaruk says, "but you'll also get motor activity of the arms and hands, as well as sensory input from them." To get clean data, he needed to find someone able to achieve orgasm without touching herself.

Vicky—not her real name—is one of these women. A California college student, she can climax by "thinking off." She contacted Komisaruk after hearing about his work from one of his other test subjects at a party.

"It's amusing to tell people that I jack off in an fMRI for science," says Vicky, quickly adding that the process is more like work than sex. A typical day of research begins with Vicky lying on the fMRI machine's bed; Komisaruk and his team strap down her head. Then she's fed into the doughnut and the machine begins taking pictures, a process Vicky describes as "loud and clunky." She stimulates herself by contracting her vaginal muscles rhythmically and controlling her breathing for twenty-six minutes.

Vicky and the imaging team worked out a hand signal she can flash when she starts to orgasm. "Basically, my head was strapped to a board in an extremely loud machine, and I had to let them know when I was about to come, so they could mark it on the computer," she says, laughing. "Whoo—so sexy!"

"We got excellent data from her," Komisaruk says, adding that Vicky is one of twelve women in his study who can "think off." "Because there is no distraction related to movements and sensory input from arms and hands," he explains, "it illuminates the brain activity involved in producing the orgasm." Certain brain regions really stand out once the noise is eliminated: For example, the nucleus accumbens, associated with the brain's reward system, turns out to be a big player in orgasm. There is also heightened activity in the anterior cingulate cortex, which is linked to pleasure, pain, and craving; and in the amygdala and the hypothalamus, areas that process emotion. "Orgasm is probably incredibly good for the brain," Komisaruk says. "The entire organ is being oxygenated."

At the other extreme are research subjects who were thought to be unable to reach orgasm at all. In the early 1990s a colleague of Komisaruk's, Rutgers professor Beverly Whipple, began a series of studies on women whose spinal cord injuries had left them totally numb below the waist. Many had been told by doctors that they would never orgasm through genital stimulation again, but Whipple wasn't so sure. She had come across anecdotal reports to the contrary since the '70s. "I wanted to validate the sexual responses I was seeing in paralyzed people," Whipple says. So she went to the lab.

An early version of Komisaruk's calibrated vaginal stimulator turned out to be the perfect tool for the job. Because the subjects have no sensation in their genitals, there was the slight but real possibility that they'd inadvertently hurt themselves while masturbating. But using the force-measurement readout as a guide, the scientists could see how much pressure the women were exerting and prevent them from injuring themselves.

Sure enough, some of the women experienced what seemed to be orgasms. "One woman hadn't tried stimulation for two years since her accident. She was crying and I was crying—it was very moving," Whipple says. The conventional wisdom held that these were "phantom orgasms"—more like a memory or a dream than the real deal. But Whipple and Komisaruk had an alternative explanation: that the anatomy textbooks—which had all the vaginal nerves routing to the brain via the spine—were wrong. "I hypothesized that the vagus nerves"—which travel up the front of the body—"bring sensory input from the G-spot and the cervix to the brain," Komisaruk says, "bypassing the spinal cord."

To test the theory, they turned to the magnet, comparing the so-called phantom orgasms of paralyzed women with the orgasms of ambulatory women. They got a match. "Even though they could not feel the stimulus in their genitals," Whipple explains, "they had orgasmic response in the same area of the brain as women without spinal cord injury. These were not imaginary orgasms. They were real." Whipple and Komisaruk had fMRI proof, the scientific equivalent of a smoking gun.

Komisaruk's grad student, Breen, continues to investigate the vagus nerve. Not only is it a pathway to orgasm; it might also modulate pain signals. I learn this the hard way.

I'm messing with the vaginal stimulator when Breen shows me another contraption. "Analgesy meter" is stenciled across its side. "It's used to measure pain," Breen explains.

Though she never offers to let me test-drive the tampon, Breen suggests I give the analgesy meter a spin. It looks sort of like an old-fashioned postal scale, except instead of a little dish for your mail there's a piece of pointed plastic with a cap on it. The soft part of my finger rests on the pointed bit, and the cap presses down on my nail. As Breen moves a slider that goes from one to twenty, my finger is pushed down harder and harder. "Tell me when it gets to be too much," she says.

It reaches about thirteen before I yelp. "OK, too much!"

Breen's eyes are shining. "One of the things Dr. Komisaruk discovered is that women who are stimulating the anterior vaginal wall can take 50 percent more pain than they can when they're not," she tells me excitedly. "If they have an orgasm, their pain threshold rises 100 percent."

Unfortunately I'm neither stimulating nor orgasming and my finger is still squashed. "Could you take my finger out, please?" I gurgle.

"Oh, sorry!" Breen says, releasing me and warming again to the topic. Her doctoral work indicates that a woman with lingering soreness from a back injury can get up to a full day's relief by using the stimulator once a day for several minutes.

Komisaruk and Breen hope someday to develop a painkiller

based on this quirk of the female body. Komisaruk has even patented a small sequence of amino acids associated with the pain-dimming effects of vaginal stimulation. "In rats we've determined that our analgesic is more effective than morphine," he says.

A new drug for pain is great, but I'm looking for orgasm in a bottle. When am I going to get my pleasure pill, and how will it work? The person with the big picture, and with the closest thing to an answer, is Gemma O'Brien. Perhaps the only orgasm theorist in the world, O'Brien is an Australian biomedical researcher at the University of New England in New South Wales; she has spent the last decade tracking down every study available on orgasm and the brain. She has a kind of unified field theory of female orgasm, summed up by an elaborate Venn diagram. Its three overlapping circles represent emotion, pleasure, and euphoria, along with their associated hormones and regions of the brain.

O'Brien is convinced that there's no reason why women shouldn't be as sexually satisfied as men. Because orgasmic brains look nearly the same across gender lines, she believes that inorgasmic women may be suffering due to early social experiences. Sexually repressive environments "may affect the growth of brain pathways in girls," she says.

O'Brien suggests that there may also be a genetic reason why certain women enjoy sex less than others. Just as some people experience depression because their brains reabsorb too much serotonin, some may feel less sexually charged because their brains reabsorb too much oxytocin or dopamine. Researchers could "provide a fix for that with drugs," she says, sketching out plans for a pill that keeps the oxytocin from getting absorbed too quickly. If the fix works, "you might experience bliss instead of having just an okay sort of time."

Andreas Bartels, a brain researcher at the Max Planck Institute for Biological Cybernetics in Tübingen, Germany, has done research that seems to back up O'Brien's theory. He's imaged the brains of women thinking about their sex partners. Bartels says the hypothalamus appears to be a key indicator of romantic love, and it's also a main area in the brain where oxytocin is absorbed. The chemical is released during orgasm and other sorts of mating rituals.

"Love is just a biological mechanism," Bartels says with a laugh. He's certain that a drug that tinkers with oxytocin isn't far down the road. "You can inject an animal with oxytocin and make it pair-bond with a stranger," he says. "All we need to do is apply it to humans."

Most experts believe a truly effective aphrodisiac for women will hit the market in the next decade. Meanwhile, researchers are following new neural pathways and disproving the conventional medical wisdom about orgasm. They're investigating regions of the brain whose paradoxical roles as pleasure enhancers and pain modulators may yield more than one kind of drug. Komisaruk is even suggesting a technological fix for arousal problems—a neuro-biofeedback machine that could help women learn to be superorgasmic.

The future can't come soon enough.

Romancers and Raincoaters
Susie Bright

Recently, I attended a romance novel convention in St. Louis called the Romantic Times Booklovers Convention. I joked that I was going where pornographers fear to tread—but I was closer to the truth that I suspected.

I was asked to speak about erotica—an unprecedented invitation coming from an organization of romance writers. Even though romancers know that their genre is soaking in sex, the public impression is that romance is for ladies, while "erotica" is for hussies.

But the Romantic Hussies are getting brazen. Sex *is* what drives the romance field. That's where I came in. I was on a panel with Robin Schone, M. J. Rose, Jacqueline Deval, and Laurel K. Hamilton.

Before I arrived, I quizzed Robin to explain the romance jargon to me. Romance writers have dozens of terms to describe their subgenres. There's *Sizzling*, *Spicy*, *Sensual*, and *Sweet*—to name a few—and their meanings are just as distinct as the porn terms *Gonzo*, *Pro-Am*, and *Classic*.

Because romances are written so tightly to genre, and the predictability factor is so important to their buyers, their authors can't overhaul their image too much. The explicitness of the sex scenes is the only wiggle room they have. Now that every sexual taboo has been broken, they're a little anxious, because if they add any note of realism or literary feeling, their books won't be "romances" anymore and the genre will crack. It already has.

When a woman buys a traditional romance, it's like a hardcore porn fan buying a XXX video. She wants her money shot. She does not want distractions. She wants familiarity, she wants to connect with the childhood masturbatory feeling, as my friend and offbeat romanticist Pam Rosenthal so perfectly described it to me. I say this with the utmost sympathy, but fans would probably feel exposed by that description. Still, I believe romances are stroke books—they are not so much read as used. The tension between erotica and romance isn't about sex; it's about writing style. Romance publishers are dishing out hard core. Romances have fisting scenes, and gay couples as major characters. They are overt about interracial sex, rape, S/M, incest, and every other top-ten American taboo. Harlequin and other publishers are not shy about finding out *exactly* what their readers want; they're notorious for their focus groups.

Let me examine one of these desires as an example: interracial relationships. Even though this is an exploding statistic in American life, interracial relationships are still frowned upon—to say the least. They are rarely discussed outside the alternative media. In the mainstream, there's nothing except a few Hollywood celebrities who are held up as a lofty ideal. In real life, when it's happening to *you,* there are confrontations with various racist hysterics and ultimatums from your family, who swear they'll never accept you, never speak to you again, etc. etc. Of course, sometimes it works out for the best, but those of you with multicultural families know what I'm talking about! We are not supported by the mainstream media or institutions.

However, in Romance World, the heroine is frequently in bed with someone of a different color. White women with black men, and black women with white men—this is a hot ticket. This year, "Mr. Romance" was black and most of the attendees were white. The specialty line of romances marketed to black women is also filled with these couplings, which would be a total scandal in black literary circles. As in all romances, these love couplings occur in completely unrealistic stories where the beauty and nobility triumph—aided by pots and pots of juicy lust.

Another romance fetish is overt bondage and domination/submission. Rape-like or forced sex is terribly popular. By comparison, "porno" has become more politically correct over the decades. The mainstream stuff that you see on cable TV avoids the above-mentioned taboos, and the videos that focus on such material keep as low a profile as the naughty romances do.

The next time you prepare to be scandalized by a degrading bimbofest in an X-rated DVD, please consider that the identical thing is being described, from a female perspective, in romances. It's just that the objectification happens in the opposite direction.

You know how, in porn, the women's bodies are the ones that always have to be perfect, while the men can be kinda droopy or overweight? In romance, it's the reverse. The men's bodies are all *pumped;* the women can be—whatever. Her imperfections are irrelevant, or sympathetic; but the hero has to be an oiled studmuffin. Fabio is Jenna is Fabio.

The biggest difference between my *Best American Erotica* and one of the "Sexxxy" romances isn't the sex—it's the style of the writing: literary fiction vs. genre. Every romance has a happy, monogamous ending, while *Best American Erotica* stories are more diverse, offering no such guarantee.

In the same way that sci-fi and mystery novels have become more psychological and complicated, romance—which has remained the infantile genre for the longest time—is maturing. Women still love their romances—the way they love their Barbie Dolls—but they're buying other things now, too.

Romance readers are not remaining "monogamous" in their tastes; their reading interests are diversifying. Even the readers of inspirational (that is, Christian) romances read the sexy titles, too. Romance is losing readers to Chick Lit and to mainstream women's fiction. Those readers are the types who are apt to like erotic literary fiction as well.

Military stories, thrillers, and mystery/PI/cop stories are making a big splash too—another example of fusion. The most interesting writers I interviewed were a group of female Vietnam vets who turned to writing. There were lots of PIs, cops, retired cops, cops' wives, etc.

One exception to the Dowdy Look at the conference was the Goth-vampire crowd, which is openly into S/M. They were few in number but visible. Laurel Hamilton personifies this group. She appeared in a corset, accompanied by bodyguards who were also in corsets. She offered sex-positive encouragements one minute but made protective, conservative warnings the next. She is in favor of S/M explorations but against what she called "casual" sex. She is delighted to investigate kinky practices for her stories, but she warned her fans not to look at the Web pages she'd devoured in her research. I've never heard an author try to protect her fans like this before, while simultaneously titillating them. You'd never hear John Grisham tell his fans, "You'd better not look at the legal files I've seen; they'd be too much—but wow, I can't wait to show you my racy version."

I have no dispute with the romancers about sex—I appreciate their unapologetic fantasy life. It's funny, no one finds it "dangerous" when women have taboo fantasies, only when men do. There's this sense that women have realistic boundaries, no matter how cockamamie their fantasy life may be. But if a man reveals a taboo fantasy, everyone assumes that he's about to run out and perform it.

No, what I found myself advising the conference was rather contrarian—it was about writing, not about sex. I urged the authors with ambivalence about writing romance novels to abandon ship—to abandon genre writing altogether. When these writers find themselves in struggles with editors and agents over "formula," I'd ask them to realize the stakes. If they break with the formula, they'll be better writers. There is no literary future in subservience to clichés. The commercial choice, to go with formulaic demands, may or may not prove to be a moneymaker. You can't count on it. Frankly, I don't know what path leads to superstardom in romance.

I do know this: if you write authentic, emotionally truthful, graceful prose, you won't experience a moment of artistic regret—and you'll have a reputation you won't have to put a corset on to defend!

Tortured Logic
Eli Sanders

The Bush White House Fights for the Right to Continue Torturing Prisoners in U.S. Custody While the Bush Justice Department Prosecutes Pornographers Who Depict Torture. Welcome to the New War on Porn.

Here is how Max Hardcore makes his living: He rams his cock into women's mouths until they vomit, and then he sells videos of the encounters. He sells other videos, too, videos that feature his signature contribution to the world of hard-core pornography: a flexible rubber tube that allows women to suck from their own asses the semen or urine he has just deposited there, often very roughly. Are you turned on yet? Hardcore has been accused (but not convicted) of raping a British porn star named Felicity. He also has been accused of misogyny, a charge that seems apt given that many of his videos feature him shouting degrading insults at the women (often dressed as schoolgirls, complete with pigtails and hairless vaginas) who appear in his films. He describes himself as "an American original" and a leader in the field of "sexual mistreatment," and in addition to his novel use of rubber tubing, he claims both to have pioneered the practice of "anal gaping" and to be at the vanguard of "the misuse of medical speculums."

Will the culture suffer in the slightest if this man is prosecuted for obscenity? We may soon find out.

On October 5, 2005, agents of the FBI raided Hardcore's Los Angeles studio as part of a federal obscenity investigation, seizing the servers for his website and showing particular interest in five Hardcore videos: *Pure Max #16, Max Hardcore Fists of Fury #3, Max Hardcore Extreme Schoolgirls #6, Max Hardcore Golden Guzzlers #5,* and *Max Hardcore Golden Guzzlers #6.*

To many whose livelihoods are directly or indirectly tied to America's $20-billion-a-year porn video industry, the timing of the raid made it seem like an opening shot in a wider war on smut. A few months previous, Attorney General Alberto Gonzales had announced the formation of a new squad of Justice Department officials dedicated to "the aggressive and effective prosecution of those who create, sell, and distribute obscenity." The move provoked laughs among some within the FBI, with one anonymous agent sarcastically telling the *Washington Post*: "I guess this means we've won the war on terror." But Gonzales, at the time being mentioned as a possible Supreme Court pick, and perhaps needing to shore up his conservative bona fides in case he was tapped by President Bush to head for the high court, appeared serious. A memo to FBI agents, obtained by the *Washington Post,* counseled that the best odds for convictions on obscenity charges would involve pornography that "includes bestiality, urination, defecation, as well as sadistic and masochistic behavior." The memo appeared to cover such a wide swath of territory that it sent shivers through the large community of pornographers who, while they may find Max Hardcore's work to be coarse and disgusting, make their own livings producing pornography that includes tamer depictions of rough sex and bondage. As a result, a number of bondage and S/M websites have now gone dark or begun self-censoring in order to avoid potential prosecution.

"Everybody's living in fear," said one Seattle-area S/M website operator, who asked not to be named out of concern that it might draw the attention of federal investigators.

Ironically, the behaviors described as prosecutable and obscene in the FBI memo overlap quite directly with behaviors that FBI agents and others have witnessed at U.S. facilities holding prisoners in the War on Terror. At these facilities, actual torture—not adults hurting each other for sexual pleasure, but adults torturing other adults in order to coerce confessions—has reportedly occurred. Pictures have surfaced showing U.S. soldiers engaging in a level of brutality that makes the brutality dished out by Max Hardcore seem gentle in comparison. And at the U.S. prison camp at Guantánamo Bay, Cuba, an FBI agent has reported seeing prisoners "chained hand and foot in a fetal position to the floor, with no chair, food, or water. Most times they had urinated or defecated on themselves, and had been left there for eighteen to twenty-four hours or more." One had pulled his own hair out so that it lay in a pile on the floor next to him. Even more ironically, it was Gonzales who, in 2002, as White House Counsel, signed off on a memo widening the possibilities for violent behavior by U.S. interrogators, a memo that led directly to Americans viewing, in pictures from Abu Ghraib and reports from Guantánamo Bay, the sadism, urination, and defecation that Gonzales appears to abhor so greatly in another context.

And still more ironically, top Bush administration officials have been fiercely lobbying against a move by Senator John McCain to outlaw any further torture of prisoners held by the United States, with Vice President Dick Cheney emerging as the most prominent and passionate administration defender of torture. Meanwhile, American conservatives have responded positively to Gonzales's move to curtail the sadistic porn available to Americans, with the Family Research Council announcing "a growing sense of confidence in our new attorney general" as a result of the new obscenity squad.

The Justice Department says it has not kept track of obscenity investigations by the squad since it was formed, but the National Coalition for Sexual Freedom says the FBI has wasted little time in acting on its new directive. Three websites, including Max Hardcore's, have been targeted since the antiobscenity squad came into existence, according to the NCSF. That brings the total number of obscenity cases brought under the Bush administration to sixty, the organization says. During the Clinton years, there were only four.

It's difficult to find people, even within the porn industry, who are willing to rally behind the three websites that have been targeted since the obscenity squad was formed. Max Hardcore's site still peddles his trademark "sexual mistreatment." NowThatsFuckedUp.com, another targeted site, offered free porn to U.S. soldiers in exchange for photos of dead Iraqis—until its operator was arrested by local authorities and charged with over three hundred counts of obscenity. (Though local authorities are responsible for that investigation, the NCSF believes it was inspired by the new federal emphasis on obscenity prosecutions.) And Red-Rose-Stories.com, the third targeted site, allegedly trafficked in written accounts of pedophilia (or "intergenerational stories," as

Susan Wright, spokeswoman for the NCSF, prefers to put it) until the FBI took the site's computers and threatened its operator with obscenity charges.

Of more concern to people in the industry than the continued viability of those three sites is the chilling effect that may be produced by prosecuting people on the sadistic fringe, and the slippery slope that could result if the Justice Department is able to make an obscenity charge against Max Hardcore stick.

Wright admits Hardcore's site is extreme, but she adds: "That's why they're going after it. They get a successful prosecution, and they can go onto someone else."

The Justice Department doesn't exactly dispute this notion.

"The formation of the obscenity taskforce serves as a very visible sign that the department is making a renewed effort to enforce these laws," said Paul Bresson, a department spokesman.

So who might be next? Many in the mainstream bondage, dominance, and sadomasochism community say they're not willing to wait to find out.

"I know lots of people who have simply gone out of business because they are so afraid of the law," said Lydia McLane, a professional dominatrix based in Seattle, who is now reviewing some of the images on her website for fear they could be thought to constitute obscenity. "There's no definition of obscene. They're not going to be able to define it properly, so there's going to have to be test cases, and a lot of people are simply unwilling to be test cases."

Indeed, insex.com, a bondage and S/M website operated by Intersec Interactive Inc., has announced it is looking for a foreign buyer because "continuing to produce insex.com from the U.S. would be too great a potential liability."

It's a way around U.S. law that a number of operators of similar U.S. websites have said they are considering. A statement on Intersec's website explained: "While Intersec is certain that a potential prosecution would have no chance of success...the staff is unwilling to fight a lengthy and expensive court battle only to emerge victorious but bankrupt."

Other sites that don't have the name recognition or financial wherewithal to justify relocation, such as grandpadesade.com, which operated four low-budget S/M websites, have announced they will simply give up rather than try to go forward in the current climate.

"We did not receive any money," the grandpadesade.com site now states. "In fact I have never made a single cent from the lifestyle. We did not have anything about kids, dead bodies, beasts, or other such things. There was nudity and there were codes to prevent kids from viewing the material and we signed up for the major child protection programs and porn blocking programs.... These sites were about education, answering questions, and just fun. Now they are gone and you ask why? Well, it seems anything to do with S/M is thought of as porno by the Bush dictatorship.... Until the U.S. comes back to its senses, and stops these holier than thou folks, we will stay dark."

Subnation, another site that describes itself as primarily educational, posted a similar decision. "I am afraid that the current climate of intolerance and persecution by the FBI has forced me to reconsider whether or not to continue," the site operator wrote. "While I am not worried about my own situation, I must be mindful of what effect any possible prosecution could have on other family members. For that reason I have decided to discontinue this site."

Still other sites are, like McLane's, trying to stay in safe territory by modifying or removing certain images. The popular site suicidegirls.com recently announced it was removing images "with fake blood and any images we felt could be wrongfully construed as sadist or masochist," out of a desire to "ensure that we are not targeted by the U.S. government's new war on porn."

If part of the Justice Department's goal in creating the obscenity taskforce was to send a "very visible" warning to the wider S/M community, it seems it has already succeeded.

Proving obscenity in this country is not an easy business. The U.S. Supreme Court has long tried to define where free speech ends and obscene speech begins, a history that former Chief Justice Warren Burger described as "somewhat tortured" in the majority opinion in the most recent obscenity case to make it to the high court, *Miller v. California.* In that case, decided in 1973, the Supreme Court overturned the obscenity conviction of a California man, Marvin Miller, who had been mass-mailing adult brochures throughout the state, including to a restaurant in Newport Beach, California, where the restaurant manager and his mother one day opened their mail and discovered brochures from Miller advertising books titled, among other things, *Sex Orgies Illustrated* and *An Illustrated History of Pornography.* The restaurant owner and his mother had not requested the brochures, were not happy to receive them, and made this known to local police. And that, ultimately, led to Miller's prosecution and conviction for distributing obscenity.

In overturning Miller's conviction, Justice Burger and a majority of the 1973 court created a multipart test for obscenity that still stands today. "Obscene material is not protected by the First Amendment," it begins, upholding previous Supreme Court rulings. But, outlining the new test, it goes on to say that obscene work may only "be subject to state regulation where that work, taken as a whole, appeals to the prurient interest in sex," is "patently offensive," and "does not have serious literary, artistic, political, or scientific value." The standard for determining whether something is "prurient" was set as being what "the average person, applying contemporary community standards" would think.

The decision, critics have argued, creates uneven enforcement of obscenity laws from community to community, and provides an incentive for federal prosecutors to bring cases in conservative communities that could not be brought elsewhere. More importantly, argues the NCSF, the test has been rendered obsolete by the advent of the Internet. To which community's standards is a website like Max Hardcore's now held? The community standards of LA, where it is based? Or those of Wichita, where it can just as easily be viewed? A lawsuit over whether the Miller test, in the online age, unfairly makes everyone in America responsible to the nation's most conservative community standards, wherever those conservative standards may currently reside, is now on appeal—and, some believe, headed for the Supreme Court.

Until then, the question remains: Is what Max Hardcore does obscene? And if so, what does it mean for the wide spectrum of sexual behaviors that lie somewhere between sucking someone else's piss out of your own ass through a rubber tube and, say, the missionary position?

"Everybody's worried because they don't know where it's going, and that's obviously what their objective was," said the Seattle area S/M pornographer who asked not to be identified. He predicted that all pornographers would suffer from an expanded Justice Department crackdown, "except the big guys, who can afford to fight it."

The "big guys," this pornographer and others pointed out, these days include Rupert Murdoch's News Corporation and the General Motors Investment Management Corporation, which together own a large part of DIRECTV, a company that beams pornography to hotel and home televisions via satellite. Hotel chains, such as Sheraton, Hilton, Marriott, and Hyatt, and Time Warner Incorporated also make considerable money from selling pornography, the *Washington Post* has noted. None of them appear to be on the Justice Department's hit list, yet.

"They're just going for the easy targets," complained the local S/M pornographer. "Nobody's going to touch Marriott Hotel chain, General Motors, and all that bunch."

Russell Harmon, who with the help of his wife, his girlfriend, and his wife's girlfriend runs the local bondage site twobigmeanies.com, said that, as a small operation, Two Big Meanies can't take the risk of not self-censoring. "We did a shoot that involved play with needles that we're just sitting on, that we're not going to use," he said. They're also obscuring genitalia on their website and cutting portions of videos in which people sound like they might not be having fun.

"There's the idea of a sort of government monopoly on violence," Harmon complains, trying to figure out the rationale behind the administration's simultaneous defense of torture and prosecution of depictions of consensual rough sex play. "The other idea is, if you have a sexually repressed populace, they're a lot easier to keep frightened. It's important, in a fascist society, to keep people sexually repressed. That makes the politics of control easier."

The anonymous local pornographer recalled a former client of his website, a soldier who recently died in Iraq and whose sister called after his death to cancel his account. "He was fighting for the right of Americans to be free to live their lives, so long as they didn't harm others," he said bitterly. "And basically the administration was shooting him in the back while he was over there fighting."

The idea that the freedom to depict hard-core sex is an inalienable American right is one argument for letting Max Hardcore and others be. A more pragmatic argument is purely economic—it's about a predicted transfer of American porn profits to other, more tolerant countries, given the impossibility of stamping out kinky desires here.

"I don't know what these clowns think they're trying to achieve," he said. "If [kinky porn production] moves to Holland, do they actually think Americans are going to stop downloading kink?"

But most, like Harmon, return in the end to the slippery slope argument. "If they close down," he said, speaking of a site called pissmops.com that he says recently went dark in response to the new obscenity squad, "what closes down next?"

Where the Truth Lies
Emily DePrang

About four months ago, I was fired for sexual harassment. The management dubbed this "mutually agreeable," which is corporatespeak for "Don't let the door hit you in the ass on the way out." The way I see it, I was fired for being a lesbian.

My sexuality has always been a topic of conversation among friends and strangers. It just comes up. I can't be bothered with chaste silence or pronoun switching. This is how I came to be known as The Lesbian on the second day of my new job at a place we'll call Last Chance Loans.

The office seemed friendly enough. The dress code was jeans; the CEO's dachshund waddled down the hallways. I felt comfortable right away. LCL was peopled with characters like Dina, a wiry forty-year-old who once stuck her head in my cubicle to say, "I don't like Jessica Simpson. She looks like she smells." The following is an actual transcript of my coming-out conversation with Dina.

Me: "Blah blah blah I'm a lesbian."

Her: "Oh, I *love* Melissa Etheridge!"

Then she asked what I thought of the Catholic priest scandal. "I mean," she said, "the Church seems to attract a lot of them."

"A lot of whom?" I asked.

"The gay men."

"Um," I said, "those priests weren't gay men. They were pedophiles. It's different."

"Oh yes," she said, nodding gravely. "That's a lot worse."

Then there was Jane. I figured any place that hired Jane as its receptionist couldn't be all bad. She was young and awkward, with a slight sneer and the deadpan delivery of Steven Wright. I liked her duck-footed swagger and ill-fitting button-up shirts with boy-beaters peeking out. Between Jane and Deirdre, a snarky twenty-something who flashed her middle finger at me at least once a day, I thought I'd found my work buddies.

We took three smoke breaks a day together to warm up in the sun and joke about our coworkers: Clara, the ferociously ambitious, slightly hunchbacked executive assistant; my boss, the marketing director who sauntered in late every Monday; the office manager/grandmother who carried an illegal seven-inch switchblade in her purse. I told them about my exchange with Dina and they fell over laughing.

One day, I noticed a rainbow-studded ring on Jane's hand. "Is that a pride ring?" I asked.

"Nah," she said. "I got it in New Mexico."

"Now, are you sure you're not a dyke?" I teased, "Because you wear boybeater shirts every day."

"Is that a gay thing?" Deirdre asked.

"Yeah, we invented that," I said. "Y'all straight girls steal all our best stuff."

"Huh," said Jane and Deirdre. Our conversation moved on to something else.

A week later, the human resources director called me into her office.

Six years ago, when I was an office assistant in the math department at the University of Texas, a handsome thirtysomething professor would trot into the mailroom like a yellow Labrador whenever I lingered there. He'd stare at me and make coy conversation. I liked his warmth and attention, his sandy hair and radical politics. One day, he invited me to his office for tea. He brewed me a cup of Tazo that turned deep red. "It's called Passion," he said with a grin. Then he showed me a book of letters exchanged between Napoleon and Josephine. He read aloud a passage describing her pubic hairs as a dark forest in which he wanted to get lost.

I smiled and laughed. What was I supposed to do? I was a virgin, a freshman, and a girl who had been taught that it was vain to assume someone was hitting on her. I knew his behavior was weird, but he wasn't hurting me. It wasn't until he started e-mailing me (without having asked for my e-mail address) and calling my dorm room (without having asked for my number) that I got creeped out. He asked me to the movies. I declined. He asked me again, and I mentioned it to my supervisor.

After that, we still worked in the same department, but his entrances and exits were rushed and angry. I spent the rest of the year feeling like a heel for getting him in trouble, however informal. I told myself that I was just looking for attention, playing the victim, that I should have been able to dissuade him by myself.

But the fact that *you don't feel that you can say no* is the exact reason sexual harassment policies exist. It wasn't until years later that I accepted how young eighteen is and how skeevy his juvenile advances were. I stopped feeling guilty for tattling on him. The part of the experience I'll never forget is how hard it was for me to say anything—to say no to him, and to say "Um…" to my boss.

At a later job, a supervisor asked me out on a date and was boyishly disappointed when I declined. I worked there for another year and we never shared a moment's discomfort. Though his asking may have been technically inappropriate, I never would have filed a complaint, because I didn't feel harassed. However meticulous my employers' definition of sexual harassment—and every employer of mine has had one—my definition has always come down to *Am I queasy as I step into the elevator? Do I want to object but stop myself out of embarrassment and self-doubt? Am I scared?*

When I was hired at Last Chance Loans, part of my induction was a grave-faced and long-winded explanation of their sexual harassment policy. As the human resources director read me the list of potential offenses, I imagined a balding, suited, leering man committing them: the ass slap, the crotch cup, the lewd comment about wanting to fuck famous women, the needless brush of the passing groin, the inquiries about my sex life. (As a waitress, I got this all the time. The most colorful comment came from an elderly sonofabitch who asked, as I refilled his coffee, "What do you girls do, anyway? Bump tacos and giggle?") How I hated the hypothetical sexist bastard—he'd never mess with this dyke! I nodded along with Ms. HR, glad to know that her hard-ass policy would have my back if I ever needed it.

When I got the call, I walked into the HR director's office with confidence. I'd been there only a month but had quickly determined that it didn't take much to impress my employers. When I alphabetized my boss's files, she treated me like a genius. So why did Ms. HR have the steady eye of a cobra with a spreading hood?

"Shut the door, please," she said.

Oh shit. I sat down and folded my already clammy hands.

"There have been some issues brought to my attention and I want to discuss them with you." She pulled a manila folder out of her desk and opened it.

I got very still, as prey tend to do.

"I see that you did a cartwheel in the lobby?" she said.

I relaxed. So I was going to get called out for being a dumbass. That was fair. "I'm sorry," I said with a little laugh. "It's just that I have to pee all the time, and I have to pass Jane to get to the bathroom, so it gets embarrassing. I try to do something to distract her from actually keeping count. The lobby was empty, but that was dumb. I apologize."

Ms. HR didn't look up. "I see also that you flashed her?"

"No!" I yelped, recoiling as if bitten. "No! I would never do that. No, I…I think I may have acted like I was going to—like, mimed it? But I never did…"

"But you acted like you were going to," she countered.

I was struck dumb. Was that the same as doing it?

Ms. HR continued. "I see here you also asked her about a pride ring, and implied that there was something lesbian about her T-shirts."

I began to tremble. How did she know about our talks outside? Someone must have told her. But who? And why?

"But…those were jokes I made outside the office."

"We take sexual harassment very seriously here at Last Chance Loans," she replied.

The balding man was back in my head.

The balding man was me.

The inside of my chest started to crumble.

"Also, you told Clara she was…'fine'?" Ms. HR queried.

I remembered that day. All the bigwigs were at a conference, so work ground to a halt. The women of the office had gathered to sit in the sun and gossip. It was right after our secretary had declared herself "a straight-up black Bronx bitch." We had a new girl in the office who was enjoying the joviality. Clara walked in, and I introduced her in my best *Ladies' Man* voice: "That's Clara. She fine!"

"I...I..." I stuttered.

"And when asking to be transferred to Jane," Ms. HR continued, "you were asked, 'Do you want Jane?' and you said, 'All the time.' "

"On the phone!" I exploded. "To *talk* with!"

I was starting to panic. How many people had complaints about me? Had she conducted an investigation prompted by one complaint, or had they each come to her individually? Had my coworkers compared notes in the copy room in hushed tones? Did they feel about me as I'd felt about my math professor?

"Look," I said, clinging to my dignity. "Clearly, I've misinterpreted the office environment. But shouldn't I have been given some kind of warning?"

"Consider this your warning," she said.

"But," I pressed, "if I'd known I was being misinterpreted, I could have adjusted my behavior."

"*Do* you think you can adjust your behavior?" she asked, leaning forward. "Is that something you think you can change?"

"Of course!" I cried. I searched her eyes for some sign that she knew this was absurd, that it was a corporate exercise, perfunctory, that she was just doing her job. But her unblinking composure veiled a blend of disgust and pleasure.

I looked at my hands. She wanted to know if I could stop terrorizing the women of my office.

I used to think I'd escaped the self-loathing that plagues most gays. I'd grown up well-loved and free of religious condemnation.

I had moved to New York City from Austin, Texas, where you can't throw a rock without hitting a lesbian. But sitting in Ms. HR's office, I felt the way I did when I got busted playing doctor with Eileen Gospel in fifth grade: that I was bad in a way so base that doors had to be closed before I could be reprimanded.

She continued. "I'll be meeting with the management to decide how to proceed. And we'll need to make your placement agency aware of the situation."

The stain grew. I wasn't just losing my job—I was losing my means to get another one. I'd have to start over. I saw her reading my file to the lazy boss who loved me, and to Andy, the jokey guy at OfficeTeam who once considered me his finest temp. I saw their faces change as they listened to her. I saw myself change in their minds. I saw Andy explaining to his bosses why my file was being terminated. And everyone, in my mind, regarded me as the plague. Sexual harassment is too dire for the benefit of the doubt. No one would associate with me now. Shit, shit, was this really happening?

Finally, I burst into tears. I was so ashamed. How could I have made my friends feel this way? It had taken me what seemed like forever to believe that a woman could want me. I felt guilty even looking at beautiful women's naked bodies when they presented themselves for my approval. I felt like I was doing something bad to them. And now I had done that bad thing to my friends, without meaning to, without even knowing it. They *did* feel the way I feared those women would feel, and they felt it at work, inescapably—I was always there, bouncing around, talking, being heedless, reckless, assuming all was well.

I sobbed into my hands. "It does…paint a picture…" I said.

"Yes, it does," Ms. HR said. She stared at me. I could have stopped, but I didn't want to. I wanted her to see me cry. I wanted to eat away her valuable time with my sobbing, instead of moving somewhere discreet and hygienic to be rocked by her accusations.

After five or six minutes, she sighed. "You can go to the bathroom to clean up if you want. I'll let Toni know you'll be a few minutes."

Now it was my turn to stare. It was three-thirty. I was wearing a mucus mask, and she expected me to finish the day? "I think I'd like to go home now," I said. I left her office, bolted for my desk, and ripped everything out of it. My coworkers stared. The new girl—who, I thought, must not have been interviewed—said, "What happened? What's wrong?" I just shook my head. Let the other bitches tell her. I grabbed all available office supplies and ran for the door. On the way out, I started to cry again.

As I fled, I saw Jane. Her eyes were wide and worried. She started to stand up at her desk, but I wouldn't look at her. Downstairs, on Madison Avenue, I collapsed in front of a store and called my best friend.

"Lily," I said, "I just got fired for sexual harassment."

"Of course you did," she said. "Wait. You're not serious."

I limped into Central Park and told her everything. As I recounted my offenses, the shame subsided. A pride ring? Cartwheels? Ten minutes later, it seemed funny. En route to my train, I called all my friends. "I'm a sexual predator!" I crowed.

"That's what you get for defecting to corporate America!" They laughed. And I did too.

But in all my merriment, something lingered. For the next week, a little voice piped up every few seconds to remind me— *You're a pervert. People who knew you were grossed out by you. People you shared cigarettes with were disturbed enough to trot downstairs and report you.* However absurd their definition of sexual harassment, I had met it. Their reports were accurate.

I've always thought that if a woman felt sexually harassed, then she was, end of story. After all, if a victim had to prove malicious intent on the part of the harasser, then only the most extreme incidents would warrant reporting. Relentless dirty joking, the casual display of porn, and other acts that would create a threatening atmosphere would be exempt.

So I was rightfully fired. But what if the "victims" were uncomfortable with me because I was gay? Was it Ms. HR's right to terminate me to satisfy her homophobia?

A few weeks after my departure, a male former coworker sent me an IM.

"I'm sorry," he said. "If I had a nickel for every time I've done the little things you got fired for, well, I'd have a shitload of nickels. But I get away with it because I'm a guy. They expect it from me."

I thanked him for his honesty and told him not to lose any sleep over it. Meanwhile I thought, *So was sexism at work, too?*

Women at work reliably talk about a few things: each others' bodies, their dating lives and/or sex lives, and the men they work with. Commiseration and coadmiration are standard. In my first week at Last Chance Loans, my boss and a peer led me into a discussion of our respective breast sizes. They bemoaned their buxom figures, admired my "more subtle" one—so perky!—and complained about the trauma of buying a bathing suit. They knew I was gay. I felt uncomfortable. But hey, you talk about what your boss brings up, especially in your first week. And the women around me talked, as women in the sterility of an office always had, about the hottest and most slippery of topics. But I didn't talk about my sex life. I was quiet when the dating discussions came around, except to reference my few ex-boyfriends. What's a gay girl to do in a straight world? Hide in the bathroom—or the closet?

I don't know how to keep everyone happy at work. The obvious answer is to apply a stringent, elaborately delineated standard to everyone equally. But is the resulting culture of paranoia that accompanies such rigorous—and ultimately unrealistic—standards worth it? Probably not. Besides, those who handle complaints always exercise their own biases in prosecution, and they always will.

There is no equality.

Not that equality shouldn't be striven for, but all told, I'd rather err of the side of women's comfort. I guess I'd rather live in a world where I can get fired for being goofy and gay than one in which my officemate can leer at Deirdre or watch girl–girl porn on his lunch break.

What I didn't know: The day I got fired, Jane ran out into the street after me—no small gesture when you're a receptionist. She didn't see me crumpled in a little ball down the block, wailing into my cell phone, but she'd looked for me. Weeks later, when she heard I'd be giving a reading, she came to see me. She wanted to tell me it wasn't her doing. She had related our discussion jokingly to coworkers; the woman I'd called "fine" had turned me in. It had snowballed from there, Jane said. She wanted to apologize.

"You know the best part?" she said.

"What?" I said.

"Everyone says that Ms. HR is a huge dyke."

We laughed and went down the block for a beer. Now, I have a job at *FHM* where I talk to beautiful women, and Jane and I are very good friends. I got fired, but I wouldn't have it any other way.

Rope Burn
Michael A. Gonzales

"I want to be your dirty whore," the middle-aged white man screams, kneeling on all fours atop the black-carpeted floor. Hanging on the bright red wall in the shape of a giant X is an ornately crafted Saint Andrew's cross; a few feet away is a leather bed with restraints and a steel dog cage big enough for a man.

A latex-suited seductress eases her stiletto heel into his soft belly as the chill of the air-conditioned dungeon raises goose pimples on the man's pale skin. Reaching for the suede flogger she'd recently purchased from Purple Passion, the cocoa-colored mistress forces her whimpering slave to understand what king of kink Marquis de Sade meant when he scribbled: Pleasure does not exist without pain. Pain and pleasure are the same emotion.

Hours afterward, the same gentleman, a prominent Park Avenue lawyer, will trade corporate war stories at '21' with his boardroom buddies and their blonde brides. Though his booty is sore from being "a bad girl," it's a secret that his Metro-North associates and their Scarsdale spouses might never understand. Of course, how does one explain paying two hundred dollars an hour to be dressed up like a Times Square hooker (raven-hued wig, crotchless panties, high-heeled boots) while a beautiful black goddess named Mistress Sonya humiliates him in a midtown lair.

Four months later, as weary holiday shoppers bustle down a Brooklyn Heights boulevard, twenty-seven year-old graduate student Sonya is still amused by the decadent memory of that summer evening. "I made him dance like a stripper, beat him with a riding crop, and then I strapped on my big black dildo," she says, giggling. She is dressed in simple jeans and button-down blouse. Sonya's voice is hypnotically musical, with her sweet Caribbean accent. "His only complaint was that the tight boots were killing his feet."

Coming from the West Indies, Sonya was raised in Brooklyn and was an honor student. "Ever since I was a teenager I've enjoyed inflicting pain and humiliating men," she confesses. "I didn't have many willing participants in high school. The term *BDSM*" (for bondage/discipline, dominance/submission, sadism/masochism) "wasn't a part of my vocabulary; back then, I didn't even know there was a name for my particular tastes."

Though no stranger myself to New York City's hedonic underground, I stare wide-eyed at this lovely contradiction of a soul sister and wonder how many other honey-voiced/bad-ass women of color are swaggering down Broadway with handcuffs stashed in their Louis Vuitton bags.

As we relax inside a Thai restaurant, I gaze at Sonya's face, with its aura of brown-skinned innocence, and find it impossible to recognize that I'm in the presence of a premier dominatrix.

A professional mistress since 2001, Sonya drifted into this taboo territory after quitting her job at the Bank of New York. "I was bored with having a 'vanilla' profession," Sonya says. "One day I was looking at the classified ads in the *Village Voice*, and I noticed one that read 'Will Train to Be a Dominatrix. No Sex Involved.' That's how I made my decision." Learning and perfecting her craft at the notorious Den of Iniquity, Sonya later decided to strike out on her own. "Most houses take half of the mistress fee per customer," Sonya says. "But I can rent a dungeon in midtown for fifty dollars and not be stressed."

Still, one of the unwritten prejudices in the sex trade, from apartment-house call girls to strippers on stage, is that black girls often get paid less. "There are some guys who try to negotiate the price, but that's out of the question," Sonya says. "I've felt some slight racism when I worked in one dungeon. The mistress refused to put my picture in any of the print ads, and then when *Fetish World* magazine expressed an interest in putting me on the cover, she turned them down."

Sonya's disarming attitude dispels the myth that doms are total, ego-driven bitches 24/7. "Most of my customers are high-powered white men," she explains. Admittedly, while Sonya is down for whatever, there are certain lines she doesn't cross. "I won't do age play, which is mommy and baby stuff. I just don't want to change a grown man's diaper while he calls me Mama. It's a shame, really, because there are some really rich men who are into that."

While there has been debate among lawmakers about whether a domina's services—which could include foot worship (while being slapped), CBT (cock and ball torture), golden showers, and various other forms of "play"—constitute prostitution, Sonya sees little ambiguity. "If I jump in a car and slap a man for five dollars, do you think a cop would arrest me for that?"

"Maybe just a simple assault charge," I joke. "But, how many of your clients are black men?"

"I do have a couple," she says, sipping from a glass of Thai iced tea. "One likes to be treated like a dog, so I take him to parties on a leash. There are many more women of color on the scene than men. Black men like to say they're freaks, but they're really not." Grabbing her crotch as though wearing a strap-on, Sonya laughs and says, "If they were, they would come over here and suck my dick. Though blacks are seen by society as sexually liberated 'animals,' nothing could be further from the truth. Black people tend to be further behind in terms of sexual freedoms."

Still, one can't help but wonder about the role race plays in measuring levels of humiliation. "I do find it easier to degrade white guys than brothers," Sonya confesses. "With black guys, I find myself holding back. There was one black guy I slapped around till his mouth started bleeding, but after seeing the blood it was hard to continue. If it had been a white guy, I would have finished."

Yet, how far is too far when it comes to the brothers? "There are a few into being fisted, others who like to be doubly penetrated. The most extreme is one guy who asked for a brown shower," Sonya recalls. "And this dude ingested every last piece. A lot of mistresses won't do them, but if I'm comfortable with the guy, it's no problem."

Although Sonya works as a pro dom, she emphasizes that there has to be a bond and a level of trust beyond the dollar sign. In addition to her private sessions, she also enjoys attending the weekly Ulterior Motives parties. "Some mistresses think you shouldn't have to pay to play, so they look down on the profession. I love what I do," she says. "A true domina is a person who is respectful, sets limits, and is constantly growing. Being a dom is not a secret life, it's who I am."

One of Mistress Sonya's "pets," Gregory McKnight (pseudonym) has served countless black dominatrices over the years.

Lounging in his book-cluttered Bronx apartment, the thirty-seven year-old can still remember the exact moment when his kink kicked in.

"I was a seventeen–year-old buying comic books when I saw the cover of an adult magazine that had a picture of a man on all fours wearing a dog collar and a gorgeous woman was holding his leash," McKnight recalls. "Something inside of me clicked. I wanted to be that guy."

In the mid-1980s, when Manhattan was considered a madcap metropolis of debauchery, Gregory began to check out spots with names like Paddles, Hellfire, and the Vault. "I was a voyeur on the scene long before I became an active submissive." Raised as a Baptist, he says, "In the beginning I felt guilt before, during, and after. Society would say that submission equals weakness, especially as a black man. So, I had much inner conflict between the natural aggressiveness of my 'vanilla' life and my desire to be submissive."

Unlike Mistress Sonya, whose participation in BDSM is both business and pleasure, Gregory is forced to play by different rules. "It's not like I can be late for work, and say I was doing a task for my mistress. This is my chosen lifestyle, but it's still frowned on by society."

For Greg, dating is another sexual land mine he tries to negotiate, though it usually blows up in his face. "I've tried to educate a few black women, but they've never understood. They hear me talk about being submissive, and they think I'm a doormat, or it's too just 'nasty' for them."

After twenty years on the scene, where Gregory has been trained to be an obedient dog (in his mind, a Labrador retriever), he still meets few other black men. "Even today, it's rare to find other submissive black men," Gregory says. "I'm submissive by nature, and if I hate anything, it's a weak woman, and women of color are some of the strongest on the planet. Their desires are my desires."

The imagery of S/M has long been a part of our popular culture landscape. I grew up enthralled by the risqué fashion portraits of Helmut Newton in '70s *Vogue* magazines and lusting after whip-wielding Jennifer Tilly in *Bound* (the debut feature directed by the Wachowski Brothers, makers of the BDSM favorite *The Matrix*). However, with the exception of dominant blaxploitation screen queens Tamara Dobson (*Cleopatra Jones*) and Pam Grier (*Jackie Brown*), bondage-accessible Ohio Players album covers, and a few porn emporium magazines (*Black Mistress Review, Black Amazon Digest*), the thrashed booty of ebony BDSM was rarely shown.

Growing up in Harlem during the '70 and '80s, I clearly remember a time when brothers and sisters didn't admit to oral sex, let alone anything wilder. Yet, as each generation rejects the taboos of its elders (as my mom likes to say, "These kids are just nasty"), that once-forbidden subject has crept into black pop culture via music, video, and films.

Today, as witnessed by Lil' Kim's trash-talking on *Dreams* ("Babyface can pay the rent and cook me five meals/mama's got the whip appeal"), Janet Jackson strapping a stranger to a chair while performing "Rope Burn" on the Velvet Room tour, raptress Eve christening her clothing line Fetish, and Halle Berry in *Catwoman* crawling across the rooftops of Gotham City looking as if her final destination should be New York's annual Black and Blue Ball, folks of color are beginning to explore their inner freak.

"But why do we have to be considered freaks?" Mistress Heart, a leading West Coast goddess and activist, argues. Even when slightly perturbed, her telephone voice is soothing as the sea. Introduced to the scene five years ago by a former boyfriend, Mistress

Heart has become the primary voice for BDSM women of color in the Bay Area.

"The people involved in this community come from all walks of life," Heart says, "but the one thing we share is a willingness to explore sexuality outside our own 'vanilla' worlds. Does that make us some kind of fiends?"

Wide awake at six A.M. California time, Miss Heart is preparing lessons for a workshop she teaches curious novices around the Bay Area. "I'm finding that there are more black people who are attracted to BDSM, but there is more to being a domina than simply snapping a whip. I suggest my students check out websites like Dark Connections and Black Beats, as well as reading *SM 101*, by Jay Wiseman. There are mistresses who are into the scene simply for the clothes, but to be a good domina one should be trained and educated."

Rejecting the traditional BDSM garb, Mistress Heart dresses in a more elegant manner that includes evening gowns and flowing robes. Conducting her sessions anywhere from community dungeons in Oakland to renovated Victorian houses in San Francisco, she says, "Whether one is being dominant or submissive, it's important to discover your niche and what kind of play your partner likes."

As the aural Valium of Enigma's "Smell of Desire" plays in the background, Miss Heart sighs. "Everything is not for everybody. Personally, I'm not interested in jumping on a man's chest and drawing blood with my heels—no matter how much he begs."

Along with Bay Area photographer Andrew Morgan, Mistress Heart founded the Women of Color Photo Project, whose mission is to teach diversity by getting the images circulated in the community. "Why is it that when I am out in the community, the images I see on BDSM websites and in printed media do not include very many people like me? I know that the wealth of ethnic diversity this area has to offer is quite outstanding, so where are all those people in our BDSM world?"

Talking to other women of color in the Bay Area, Ms. Heart found that there is "a higher level of discomfort that has to be overcome before feeling safe in being out. If people feel that they are the only one, then it takes a lot more courage to overcome that. If the majority of what we see isn't like us, then it takes a lot more to convince us to come out to play."

"What has made people of color hesitant about dedicating themselves to the BDSM community?" I ask.

"Much of the guilt comes from moral-dilemmas issues connected to religion," Miss Heart says. "There are others who have deep-seated issues that they haven't dealt with in therapy and they feel a sense of shame. There are also issues of what slavery represents in the minds of black people. I rather say *dominant* or *submissive* than *slave*. I never use the word, because it feels like [I'm referring to] someone who doesn't have a choice. In our world, choice is everything."

A Porn Valley Story
Susannah Breslin

It's possible, I suppose, I was the first woman to set out to acquire Post-Traumatic Porn Disorder. It's possible, I suppose, I went to Porn Valley searching for something of which I was not altogether aware. Now, as I look back on it, I can see, undeniably, Porn Valley and I were two of a kind. When I first met the adult movie industry, it was changing. Faced with rising competition from the unbridled, uncensored, and uncharted world of Internet pornography, born captive but raised in recent years to run free without chastisement under a series of liberal political regimes, Porn Valley was becoming far, far more extreme. Starring stunt sex acts and unprecedented multiple penetrations, pushing the parameters of sadomasochism and redefining the meaning of degradation, seeking to uncover how far humans could really go, Porn Valley was the new Wild, Wild West, a land beyond sex, where anything went.

Today, people want to know how it all happened for me, as if to test out, in their own minds, whether, with an accidental turn down a random street, with an inadvertent slip from their personal mythology, with an inexplicable shift in their neurological weather pattern, their lives could change as totally as mine did. I can only tell you that I was there, that this really happened, and that it happened to me.

You see, the first time I found myself driving into Porn Valley, I knew, for me, it wasn't about pornography. It was about whatever the opposite of death is, and it was everything that having seen my father reduced to a substance that could be snorted was not, and it was kind of like running my face into a fist just to feel something again. It was not at all similar to the night my stepmother called to tell me that my father was dead, around eleven o'clock in the evening, on January 6th, 1996. What she said was "Your father is dead," and what I told her, with a great deal of conviction, because I was at my apartment that night, sleeping, for God's sake, while my father lay fucking dying, was "No, he's not." It was as if, in the face of the worst thing I could possibly imagine, taken to the level of a caricature I simply could not comprehend, I had believed, in spite of it all, that with my words I could will my father out of death and back into living, that I could undo the impossible finality of what was already happening. But that was that, and he was gone, winked out like a light through a window, and in that moment, and only God knows which moment it was, I knew it would never get better, that it would, in the reality I was relegated to trudge through by myself, only get worse, worse than I could begin to imagine in that awful moment.

I have no idea what my stepmother said to me after that, maybe something, maybe nothing, I don't know anymore. At some point, though, she told me, "You better come and see him," and I thought, *Are you fucking kidding me?* I would rather stick the barrel of a shotgun into my mouth and splatter my brains across the wall behind me than see my father lying like a felled tree on some metal gurney, or some cement slab, or some God knows what, who knows where, with everything that had been inside him—everything that, without thinking, with some idly wandering sperm, had created me—sucked out of him, leaving behind a shell that looked like shit, that was a scrim beyond which I would never be able to see, that was the house of my father mortally imploded. And so, when I found myself heading into Porn Valley, I knew what I was after wasn't pornography, it was something else entirely, something that wasn't my father's dead body, or my stepmother's voice on the telephone, or me holding on for dear life to my own damn life. It was something else altogether.

Do you want to know what I've seen? I can tell you what I've seen. One hundred and twenty-five men having sex with one woman in one day in Van Nuys. Eighty-six men masturbating onto the face of a porn starlet kneeling on the floor of a soundstage across the street from a neighborhood park in North Hollywood. A three-foot-one-inch midget named Bridget climbing out of a suitcase to have sex with a fiftysomething British man with the nom de porn Dick Nasty in a San Fernando Valley mansion. A club in Amsterdam in which thousands and thousands of people had gathered, many of them in the dark upstairs, where they engaged in orgies with strangers as, downstairs, on the massive stages, an aqua-colored-rubber-clad dominatrix took both her fists and put them up the rear end of a heavily muscled bald man, as, across the room, on a gynecological table, a woman lay, with her feet in stirrups, so anyone in the audience could don a glove and penetrate her, as, in the backroom, a red-vinyl-clad mistress stuck a needle through the mouth of a dwarf dressed as Little Red Riding Hood upon whose breast her master had carved a heart in razor-blade-let blood. A blonde-haired girl getting gangbanged on a chintz bed-spread in Riverside—she said she did it for the fun of it—while the head of this all-male club discussed his divorce proceedings in the kitchen. Two male porn stars, their faces made up by a Hollywood special effects artist to look like zombies, double-teaming a girl in a schoolgirl uniform on the property of a junkyard in Sunland. A starlet by the name of Chloe with her arms tied behind her back in a purple V-shaped S/M sleeve explaining it didn't hurt because she was so flexible from her years of doing ballet. A man of mystery in his thirties, his body marked with artistically rendered tattoos, being tortured by a woman in a downtown LA loft before he would go on to attend a high-stakes poker tournament in Las Vegas. A Russian hanging in a cocoon from the ceiling of a dark dungeon. The African British coprophagic at a party in London. The lone sex coach in a hotel on the edge of the Pacific Ocean.

What did I do in Porn Valley? I was the one standing in the corner when the man in the middle leaned away from the girl upon whom he was performing, and he looked around the room, and he was holding himself in his hand, and I was watching him, and he was searching for something, and he found me staring at him, and that was when he smiled.

It all started—this is how it always starts, isn't it? This is how your story goes when you try to tell it. It was late 1997. I was a writer. I was on assignment. I was interviewing a porn star at a strip club in San Francisco. You may have heard of her—her name is Jenna Jameson. Her publicist had invited me to visit the set of one of her movies if I was ever in Los Angeles. Then, not long afterward, there I was. It was me, you can see, standing in the middle of a Little Tokyo parking lot on a swelteringly hot day. In front of me, one of the city's fire trucks was parked. On the fire truck, seven people were having an orgy. I was holding a pen and paper.

One of the male porn stars called out "Lube!," raised his hand into the air, and into his palm sailed what he needed. I looked to my left. I saw a line of other writers standing there to report on the day's events for magazines with names like *Cheri*. They were all men, they were all older than me, and they were all not me. I wondered what I was doing. Later, as I watched what happened when they put Jenna over a barrel while flames shot up around her, I got it. I was one of them now.

I moved to Los Angeles shortly thereafter. Today I would have to say the question is, since I have seen all these things: Who am I now? I'm not that person anymore. Or am I? I don't know. Does it matter? I think so. I remember who I was. I think of who I am. I consider how far I've come. Or so I let myself imagine. It's hard to know, when you've seen what I have seen. When you know what I know. It's hard to say when it all started. It's hard to tell the story of why I did what I did in Porn Valley. Let me try again.

It was like an XXX-version of the story about the Sweetheart of the Song Tra Bong, told by a man named Tim O'Brien. When he was in Vietnam he heard about a girl who wore culottes and a pink sweater. Her man flew her into enemy territory. She was young. She was innocent. She was fresh. Thing is, she fell in with the Green Berets. That's what she did. Sneaked out on patrol with them. Wasn't the same after that. She talked about it as if she wanted to eat that place. To have it there inside her. She had this appetite for destruction. It made her feel as if she was glowing in the dark. She didn't feel that way anywhere else. It's not bad—that's what she told them. In the end, she disappeared. Or so they said. Sometimes the soldiers thought they saw her in the jungle. Sliding through the shadows. She had crossed over to the other side. She wore a necklace made of human tongues. That's how she told her story, I suspect. She was dangerous. That's what they said. She was ready for the kill. That's how they described her. *I know*, I would like to tell her. *I know how it is when you have to die to live.*

Porn Valley is a place. Have you ever been there? It's in the San Fernando Valley but on no map, stretching all the way from Hidden Hills to The Narrows. From the top of the Santa Susana Mountains, you can see it spreading out underneath you like a girl. This is where 80 percent of the world's adult filmography is born, on its barren soundstages, in its rented mansions, on the manicured lawns of its suburban homes. This is the Other Hollywood, a business begetting over ten thousand X-rated videos a year, where thousands work every single day. They come to this territory, climbing over the Hollywood Hills, heading for Van Nuys, marching up those steps to central casting. They are reverse cowgirls, sexual missionaries, hard-core dogs, oversexed starlets, madman directors, producers gone totally wild. It is from Porn Valley that this product is funneled, to spread itself out across this country, to play itself out behind our closed doors, hidden away in our desk drawers, dancing across our glowing TV screens.

Not long ago, a man came to the town where I live. He wanted to meet me for a drink. I met him at a bar that's like an old-fashioned carousel. As you sit at this circular bar, it rotates around and around in a slow-moving circle. When this man began to speak, I crossed my legs. I can tell you what he wanted. He wanted me to go back to Porn Valley, this place whence I had come. And then he wanted me to write a book about it. He was a nice young man, with fine red hair, a good education, and a schoolteacher wife (sitting, I assumed, in a hotel not far from us known for its baroque grandeur). He discussed deals. He mentioned hundreds of thousands of dollars.

There you are, drinking your sidecar, listening to this man, trying to figure out what he wants. All the while, you are traveling in a circle, staring into your drink, noting the pair of African American gentlemen serving you and around whom you are circling. It does seem the bar is picking up speed, as if it is spinning and spinning, faster and faster. What do you do? You nod your head, you grin, you flip your hair, you are charmed. What you are bound to consider is the wisdom of running pell-mell right back to Porn Valley. This is how it happens, standing on the threshold. To save yourself, you turn to this man, and you ask him a question. You ask him of his relationship to pornography. What does he do? He shucks and jives. He will never tell you. That's it. You're gone.

I've got a Porn Valley story for you. Let's pretend I'm a porn star. Are you game? I know I am.

My name is Annie Body. I'm from Barstow, or Fresno, or some other outlying city. I had a mother, or a father—one but not the other. I was happy, or somebody left me, or I don't want to remember. I was a virgin who never dated, I was the girl everybody knew but nobody understood, I was the class slut who read her name on the bathroom wall in high school, thinking, *That's me,* noting what the words on either side of my name said about me. I forged a plan to be a star, to change my name, to reinvent myself. The month I turned eighteen, the day I left my boyfriend, the minute I saved up enough money, so I could go somewhere, so I could leave that place, a U-Haul arrived, a pickup truck pulled up, I put everything I had into the trunk of my car. I made my way along a stretch of highway toward a city with a crown at the top of its tallest tower. I became a student, a waitress, an actress. I didn't get far.

That's when I come across an ad in the local paper. I sense there is something in it that can make me bigger than I am, that can change the smallness inside me into something smaller, that can flip everything in my life, in my head, in my heart into the emotional equivalent of a Sears portrait background, all innocuous blues and Lithium swirls. I drive over the Hollywood Hills. The San Fernando Valley suits me. I experience déjà vu, my mind stumbles over something, my memory skips like a broken record. There's the building, the second-floor office, the man who says "Hello." I shake his hand. "Hi," I say. The door closes behind me. He explains the situation. Photos. Movies. Naked. Sex. XXX. If I'm not interested, don't let the door hit me where the good Lord split me.

I go down a hall, I enter a back room, I stand nude in the blinding light of a Polaroid flash illuminating the wood paneling behind me but wholly wiping out the finer details of my freckled features.

The next day, my telephone rings. It's the man from the office. (His hair is slick, his teeth are enameled, and he wears one gold chain because he likes to keep it simple.) I go to a house, a soundstage, a movie studio. I meet a director, a cameraman, a male performer. I am by no means a virgin—I did this once, but not professionally or anything. I recognize this is a surreality. I'm given a new name. I go through the motions. I am upside down, inside out, all around. The eye of the video camera does not falter in its unblinking stare. It makes no difference how far I open my legs or how deeply I bend over, how far I go outside myself or how deeply I fall inside myself—it is always there.

Afterward, I'm reminded of who I am when my new name comes out of other people's mouths on the next movie shoot, at the drugstore near where I live, at the strip club where I dance to earn extra money. I get a brand-new car, a really big apartment, a boyfriend who supports what I do, who will leave me because of what I do, who carries my suitcase so I can do what I do. My old life seems very, very far away. I have no regrets, except when I visit my mother, get depressed, or get drunk. In interviews for the dirty magazines on the covers of which I now appear, I say I do it for the sex. Sometimes I mean it. Sometimes I don't. Either way, that's what I tell them. Of course, I do it for another reason altogether. It makes me gape. This is the manner in which I go inside myself, for I can find no other way to get inside that space hidden within myself. This is who I am.

Let's pretend you watch porn. Are you willing? I hope so. Your name is John Doe. You're the typical male porn consumer, or an average businessman, or my number one fan. You see me during a business trip to Tokyo, in a hotel room with pay-per-view porno, or when you push PLAY in the privacy of your home, or as you are cruising through the hundreds of channels available to you on your big-screen TV. There I am, writ large before you, my mouth totally open, as if I am trying to tell you something. You don't know me, you think you know me, you know you could have me. You need release, you want to feel close to something, it's like this idle curiosity thing you get sometimes. You have a beautiful wife, you have an ex-girlfriend who drunk-dials you, you're divorced but you don't watch this kind of stuff, or at least not all that often.

You lie on the bed with your hands in your pants, you sit naked atop the sheets because it's not like anybody's going to walk in or anything, you shift from lying in wait to slowly stirring. My promise is companionship, true love, nothing that is clear to you. I am illuminated. I look near but seem distant, like your wife, like your career, like your brain inside your skull. At this moment, it doesn't matter, because you have something other than yourself when you see me. I am unquestioning, and that's the way you like it, because it means I am happy. I look at you from inside the boob tube, and even at this incredible remove I make you feel that you're the king of the world, the Top of the Mark, the master of your domain, because I have tits worth marrying, an ass worth saluting, a face that could make angels weep. Here I am. Miss America. The hottest chick in the universe. That girl. Any girl. The porn star next door.

I'm talking, the volume is on mute, you aren't listening. I'm half-clothed, totally naked, doing something fascinating. My head is thrown all the way back, my spine is curved like a boomerang, I make it possible for you to see my pink flesh. You think, not of the channel where wild animals run back and forth across distant tundra, eating and sexing, but of the medical channel where the bodies of people whose faces are covered with blue paper are cracked open with buzz saws and silver ice picks and into whose holes men in masks stick their arms up to their elbows. You watch me fucking, sucking, coming. You hold yourself in your hand, we grab each other, we hit a shared rhythm, galloping toward this conclusion of our long-distance relationship. You try to make it last. Alas, you cannot. As you go, you search me for a place to find purchase, for you feel, you fear, you find you are falling—through your life, between the cracks, beyond the point where you know yourself in this reenactment of intimacy you've undertaken in order to get in better touch with yourself. It lasts for a split second, a quick groan, a brief lifetime. Then it's over. Later, you forget about it. Maybe it never even happened.

The next day, you go to work with a different tie around your neck, your ex-girlfriend bangs on your door in the middle of the night, you keep to yourself. Months later, at a trade convention in Vegas, your friend informs you that while Elvis may have left the building, there are porn stars in the house. Cracking jokes, the two of you walk the adult convention floor. You see me at a booth. I am pretty, hot, unbelievable. You wait in a line, sidestepping your humiliation. Finally you stand before me. I sit with an oversized poster of myself on the table between us. I smile at you. You smile at me. I am, you realize, looking right through you. You're done.

Of course, if I were a man, I'd tell you a different story altogether about Porn Valley. I'd lean into you, I'd put my arm around you, and I'd whisper in your ear about this man I met in Porn Valley by the name of Jim Powers. What a man, I'd say, what a guy, I'd tell you, no one else quite like him, I'd explain. Then I'd lean all the way back, I'd open my eyes real wide, and I'd ask you, You wanna hear something really scary? After that, I'd tell you the story of my pal, my buddy, my best fucking friend Mr. Powers. That's the heart of darkness right there, I'd say as my lead into it, taking a shot of my whiskey.

It was the year 2000, I'd start, and I'd been around for a while. He was known for making the most obscene movies the world had ever seen, I'd say. He was a man who knew no bounds, I'd proclaim, staring into the distance as if it could tell me something, a man with no moral ground, I'd pronounce, looking at you with one raised eyebrow to see what you were thinking, a man who took no prisoners, I'd shout, getting the bartender to bring me another drink so I could stand to tell you the rest. Let me be clear, I'd announce, raising a finger into the air. This is not a war story, this is not a love story, this is a porn story. This man's mission was to find the farthest reaches of this business. He raised the bar, he had to have more, he had to know how far he could take it.

At this point, I'd get myself together and I'd ask you, You ever read that story "The Most Dangerous Game," about a big-game hunter, General Zaroff, who discovered the only game worth pursuing is human? I can tell you, I'd tell you, that's what this guy was doing. He was hunting humans. He had to be vewy, vewy quiet as he did it, I'd say, making my hands into tip-toeing bunny rabbits to show you how he did it. What did I do? I was the one who got on this man's back, who clung to this man's sides, who galloped into the great beyond with this man as my ride. His sport was bukkake, born in ancient Japan as punishment for women who strayed from the flock. What is meted out is a surplus of male stock designated to land squarely upon her. They may approach her, but they may not touch her.

I was the invisible man, lost in a forest of men, thinking I'd be but a stranger in their midst. Instead, it was as if I didn't exist. I was walking between them, I was headed to the center of the world, I was going to the middle of the universe. I sneaked up behind Powers, saw he was wearing a T-shirt that proclaimed him BEYOND THE GRAVE. I looked over his shoulder to see what he was filming. At his feet was a girl, kneeling on the floor, naked, nude, gleaming. She had a funnel around her neck, and she was covered in semen. She was the one he wanted to see if he could break. What did I see? She was fighting, and the troops were all coming, and the onslaught was ongoing. She was the last man standing, the lone private stuck in the trench, the solitary vet screwed into the foxhole.

What did I think? She was trying to figure out if she was a soldier or a coward, she wanted to know if she was strong-willed or weak of heart, she had to see if she could do what she had to do or if in the face of the Other she would fall. And let me tell you, I'd cry out, grabbing you by your lapels and pulling you in as close to me as possible, it was really something, because when I finally let myself get inside her, after all the others had her, it was as clear as a bell, it was as bright as the day, and I was in her, and I was out of her, and I *was* her. She was *right*. She was the human condition, the situation in which we are all eternally embattled, trying to decide who we are while the whole world hides from us. I was there, I'd bellow, I had a weapon in my hand, I raised it to my eye, I found my target. And then, I'd scream, You know what I did? I *shot* her.

That's what I did in Porn Valley, I'd tell you, having finished my entertainment for the evening. Then I'd get up and leave. You would think I was out of my mind. Of course, I could never tell you that story. I'm just some girl telling you the story about what happened when I went to Porn Valley.

This is the story, the true story, the real story. I went to Porn Valley because I could. I'd have to say that's why I did it. Because it was there, because there was nowhere else that wasn't everywhere, because it was everything I wasn't. I grew up in a house wallpapered in books, under the tutelage of two parents who spent their lives inside heads filled with words but could never say what they really meant, in a city of freaks, Berkeley, California, the birthplace of the feminist movement. Ironic, isn't it? I was born a girl, the problem with No Name having found its way inside me, dictating I would be its progeny. My father was a god, my mother was a monster, and I was their daughter. I grew up tall, like a skyscraper, six-foot-two on the outside, fifty feet tall on the inside. They told me I could do whatever I wanted. So, I did.

When my father left my childhood home, my heart shattered. When he left me a second time, it was his heart that exploded. When I went to Porn Valley, I was going into the heart of what I had never been able to understand, to find out what had stood between my father and me, to see what had stopped me from feeling alive after he died, to unearth what had kept me from my damned heart beating somewhere in Porn Valley. I said it wasn't about sex, I said it wasn't about pornography, I said it was about something else entirely. I lied. It was a car crash from which I could not look away, it was the Super Bowl–sized circle jerk that blew my mind, it was this *thing* no words can describe. Jesus Christ, they were amazing. My God, they were fascinating. Dear Lord, they were breathtaking. All those bodies, all those positions, all those scenes. All that moaning, all that groaning, all that caterwauling. All the lovemaking, all the making babies, all the making no sense. This was living, this was dying, this was trying. I was its witness, I was its testimony, I was its evidence. I came alive there, I became a woman there, I turned into a writer there.

I was the child of a man who wrote a book about a dead man in a failed attempt to resuscitate him, I was the child of a woman who failed to write a book about a woman who was already dead and didn't know it, I was the child born with writer's block who, for years and years, failed to write to save her own damn life. Porn Valley was Babylon, the mother of whores and the earth's abominations, and there they all were, living inside it, telling me their stories, telling me this story, telling me *my* story. The story I saw there was the truth, and, no lie, it was a story that was *alive*. I was a girl, a woman, a human being, who knew what they were doing—fucking, screwing, X-rated movies is what they were making—who sought of her own volition the most extreme things they were creating, who did the last thing her father would ever do so she could do the one thing her father could no longer do: stay alive, keep on breathing, forever writing.

So, I sit, in this front row seat at the same table where I once sat as a child across from my father, in a pink shotgun near a bend in the train tracks where, at night, I can hear the steel wheels grinding against the rails, less than a block from a river bigger than any I'd seen before. In 2003, I left Porn Valley. Today I live all the way across the country, as far away as I could think of from that land, in a city where there is no valley.

Someday, I'd like to say, I want to take my father to this river, gather his massive bulk in my arms, carry him to the banks, and walk into the water with him, humming a song about a half-crazy woman by the name of Suzanne. I'd lay my father in this bed, and I'd tell him a new story, the story of all the things I never said, the story of what I did and why I did it, the story of my life that will come after, the one I have yet to tell myself. Under the stars, in the middle of the night, at the center of my world, I'd look at my father. I'd see, one last time, his giant hands, his proud brow, his towering height, and I'd see, for once, what it was I could not see the night I turned away from him, what it was that led me to see what I would not turn away from. I'd lay my hand on his broken heart, and I'd mend it. I'd lay a kiss on his cheek, and I'd tell him I love him. I'd let my father go, and I'd watch him sink below the surface. I hope I'd see the stars reflected in it, I hope I'd come out of that river, I hope I'd keep on trying to tell the story of my life the only way I know how.

You see, the thing I learned in Porn Valley is that it's not about sex, it's not about pornography, it's about all that's *supposed* to be. It's the opposite of death, it's what I fled from, it's what was between my father and me all those years. It's about what sex is, it's about that of which pornography is a pornography, it's about what we are always searching for. Maybe it had to be a woman who would tell this kind of story, maybe it had to be me, maybe if I tell this story one more time I'll be able to say it's about *love*.

This is the end of my Porn Valley story. This is the part where I tell you that mourning is terminable. Where I reveal that that's all over for me. Where I let you know that I've left that world behind me. Only I can't do that. What I'd like to do, if I might, is take your hand in mine and stand together on the front line of Porn Valley. At the threshold of that chaos, at the very edge of what felt like my personal apocalypse, I would turn to you and ask you why I did this. Could you tell me? It would be the answer to my problems, the ending to this story, the theory that would make sense of everything that came before. If we could stand there, hand in hand, what you might tell me is this.

It was the only thing in this world that made everything better, it was the only thing in this world that made everything else fade, it was the only thing I could find that let me forget what had happened to me. But we can't do that can we? If a story is its author's child, as my parents taught me, what I can tell you of this story is this: I am this monster's mother, and this story's monster is me. It may well be that nothing about this story is terminable, that there is no way I can write an ending to it, that I will never be delivered from it.

Or, I could make up an ending for you, where I'm sitting on my back porch in the darkness, and it's as if something has left me, moving away from me in the tall grass, cutting diagonally across the yard, heading for a train in the distance, going somewhere else, and the only thing I can think is, *Asperges me.*

So, let this be my last testimony, let what I saw be what final-ly releases me, let all the things I've done that were no one's fault but my own be what delivers me from this. See, I've got another story I want to tell, a story that's about this story, and inside this story there is something else. If you listen closely, you can hear its heart beating.

Naked on the Set!
Auditioning for John Cameron Mitchell's *Shortbus*
Paul Festa

The first thing to know about me and my audition for John Cameron Mitchell's Sex Film Project is that I am not an actor. I'm not exactly a writer, either, although I've written somewhere in the neighborhood of a million words over the last nine years. I even had a literary agent, one of the best in the business. She didn't quite manage to sell my first book, or to like any of my others, and last year I found myself delisted by her agency after submitting an experimental narrative about an affair I had with a married couple, my age, who resembled my parents.

I'm one of those people in what Hedwig would describe as their late early thirties who have not quite decided what they are going to be when they grow up. I am sufficiently panicked about that fact, and enough of a supplicant to the American cinematic cult, to have submitted an audition tape for Mitchell's online cattle call to star in a legitimate movie with hard-core sex.

Mitchell's planned movie wouldn't be the first to marry artistic ambition and porn-worthy sexual explicitness. French directors in particular have been doing it for years, in movies such as *Baise-Moi* and *Pola X*. Mitchell dismisses those precedents as "de-eroticized and pretentious," and promises to do for sex in the movies what *Hedwig and the Angry Inch* did for the rock opera: reinvent it. "Why can't there be a movie that tells a strong story, is full of humor and pathos, is packed with powerful performances, and features a lot of explicit sex—hard-ons, cum and all?" ask the filmmakers on the Sex Film Project website. "We, as filmmakers, respect and love the complexity of sex and we feel it's been cinematically hijacked by people who don't."

To cast the project, Mitchell invited anyone and everyone to submit a ten-minute videotape describing a real-life sexual encounter. I made a movie about my affair with the parent figures, starring me and a couple of matching X-rated blow-up dolls. I closed the tape with a clips reel that juxtaposed snippets of my violin recitals at Juilliard, where I studied for three years in my early twenties, with an erotic video I'd made of myself shaving my head and jerking off into my shorn hair. After viewing four hundred audition entries, the filmmakers invited seventeen New Yorkers and seventeen out-of-towners, including me, for a week of callbacks. The producers gave me permission to publish my diary of the experience daily on Salon.com.

Once I arrived in New York for filming, I had voice mail from John Cameron Mitchell. I called him back immediately and, overriding an internal note of caution, asked him out for a drink. He demurred—he'd been on the phone calling out-of-towners all day and into the night, answering questions and assuaging fears, and was too tired to go out. But would I like to come over to his place?

In the 0.4 seconds it took me to answer this invitation by the director at approximately midnight, my brain processed a staggering number of moral and strategic calculations. Foremost among these concerned the absurd timing with which I had managed to find a boyfriend and fall in love with him mere days after starting work on the audition tape.

In a third-date conversation about monogamy, this twenty-five-year-old beauty and philosophy Ph.D. candidate said something wildly generous, and to my ears romantic, to the effect that while he was naturally monogamous, he wouldn't want for either of us to have sex only with each other for the rest of our lives. "That would be so limiting," he said.

It wasn't exactly carte blanche—carte grise maybe—but coupled with the fact that I had only known this person a week or so, and that I wanted so feverishly to be in John Cameron Mitchell's new movie, it seemed ample justification to continue working on the audition tape. The boyfriend even helped me make it, earning credits as "assistant director #3" and "fluffer to Mr. Festa," and played an uncredited role in which by several accounts he steals the entire movie.

But once this wave of giddiness washed away, I found myself pestered, if not plagued, by guilt. In the final days before my departure, as the reality of the audition set in, the boyfriend began to change his tune. "The thought of you having sex with someone else makes me physically sick," he said.

Guilt accompanied me to New York, and dined out on the story of not only how I planned to betray my boyfriend, but how I would mortify my parents. How would they react when they found out I'd been engaged in a vaguely literalized Oedipal investigation these past several years of my psychotherapeutic, private, and literary life?

How would the married couple, still friends of mine, react

when they found out that our affair was the subject of both my unpublished book and the audition tape I sent to JCM—incidentally, the husband's idol? Did I flatter myself to think they might be flattered? Was I operating under the delusion that everyone would forgive me my trespasses because a few motes of residual pixie dust might float their way after I returned from my glamorous week with the crew and aspiring cast of this X-rated movie?

The dilemma was complicated by my long-standing crush on John Cameron Mitchell. Ten years ago, I felt the first jolt of star-struck longing when I saw his picture on the cover of Larry Kramer's play *The Destiny of Me*. Hand pressed to chest, sensual mouth open in midsentence, his gaze aloft in a pang of youthful pathos, the actor seemed so open, so vulnerable, and so beautiful that even without my chronic problem with star-fucking, which years of therapy and fifty milligrams daily of the libidicide Zoloft have brought somewhat under control, I would have been helpless to resist him.

So how would I fare, face to face with him? If those lips wanted to kiss mine, could I refuse them? Would this be a curricular or an extracurricular kiss? Which was worse? Would I be kissing an open, vulnerable, beautiful face, or would I be kissing a director? Would I tell my boyfriend? Would I tell you?

Ten minutes past midnight, I arrived at the director's second-floor walk-up in the West Village. All the strategic and moral calculations inspired by his invitation were briskly erased as the director extended his hand, gave me a businesslike handshake, and after showing me into the cluttered living room of his one-bedroom apartment, offered me an array of nonalcoholic beverages. I opted for water in a coffee mug, which I managed to spill on the carpet and couch only three times in the next ninety minutes.

Seated beside John Cameron Mitchell on his sofa, I had some

of the typical responses to meeting a screen actor for the first time—that is, in addition to repeatedly flinging tap water all over his apartment. He's shorter than I would have imagined. How strange, I thought, that he doesn't walk around his apartment in a bloodstained fur coat and feathered blond wig, making lewd wisecracks and periodically breaking into heavily German-accented heavy metal. But there was also the thrill of recognition, that this was the same voice, the same eyes and sensual lips, the same prominent, virtually equilateral nose. Once or twice Hedwig peered out at me, and winked.

We talked about my fears, particularly the one about the boyfriend and his sudden metamorphosis from audition-video assistant director #3 to victim of somatic jealousy symptoms. The boyfriend was under the impression, I explained to the director, that as part of the filmmaking process cast members were supposed to become involved with each other, in an extraprofessional capacity, to establish a sexual and romantic relationship from which to build the movie.

The director gave me a look indicating that this was crazy talk and offered to call the boyfriend and assuage *his* fears. I dialed the boyfriend's number and handed my cell phone to the director, who spent the next several minutes talking casually about the project, saying nice things about the audition video and the boyfriend's cameo, and inviting him to call anytime if he had any concerns.

When he hung up, I realized I loved the director even more than if he'd thrown my legs up in the air and fucked me the minute I walked in the door.

Thursday afternoon, a cast of thirty-four hopefuls met at the Anthology Film Archives at the corner of 2nd Street and Second Avenue in the East Village, where we spent five hours watching each other's audition videos. After John Cameron Mitchell answered a few questions, the producer handed out three-page questionnaires that listed the thirty-four cast candidates along with four ratings: NEVER POSSIBLY, I THINK SO, DEFINITELY. With each video we were to rate the candidate based on his or her sexual attractiveness. Under each rating was room for written comments.

I understood why the filmmakers had us do this, and in fact it inspired less dread than the cast-member "dates" for which we were keeping our Friday through Sunday nights free. But as the videos started playing and people began scribbling on their ratings sheets, I began to feel almost as if I'd been duped. I'd made my video with the obvious purpose of interesting the filmmakers in me as an actor, as a storyteller, and as a sexual person. But now my peers were about to watch what I'd done and rate me based on something related but entirely more specific, which boiled down to that quintessential Internet-time courting query that my generation and adjacent ones will go to their erotic graves asking: "Hot or not?"

This was not the Academy of Motion Picture Arts and Sciences, supposedly voting on my artistic vision and technical prowess; it was three dozen peers contemplating whether they wanted my penis and other appendages penetrating their various orifices while John Cameron Mitchell's crew immortalized the images for an international audience. Had I known this, would I have devoted my video to the affair I'd had with a married couple who resembled my parents?

By the time we'd watched excerpts from all the tapes, I was exhausted. How had they screened four hundred of these? When it was over, the group had undergone a palpable change; we now knew one another. We knew who the hookers were, the sluts, the creative masturbators, the Left Coast hippies, the fallen Hassidim, the Freudian basket cases. We knew whose lover was in jail; we knew who ate his own cum. We knew who looked like a girl but knew he was a boy. We knew who had been raped as children. Some videos were better than others, but each one revealed some charisma, some presence, some poignancy. "I learned from every one of these," John said when the screening was through. "That's why you're here."

When our Thursday-afternoon screening at the Archives came to an end, we were under the powerful illusion that we were family, that we would all be working together on a vital mission, and that each of us had something to offer it. For the moment the crass and consequential aspect of rating one another's sex appeal fell to the background, as did the fact that we were not collaborating with but competing against one another, not just for a role but for John's approval, not just for John's approval but for John's love, not just for John's love, but for each other's.

Friday morning, I woke up two hours before my first audition. Shaving in the shower, wolfing down two overcooked pork chops for breakfast, riding the 2 Express from Chambers to 14th Street, hiking across town and up to the casting office on Madison Square, I chanted mantras to myself, *They like me, this is fun, this is fun, they like me, this is fun, this is fun, this is fun....*

When I arrived, three or four guys were loafing in the waiting room. We made small talk; in the lulls I silently practiced my mantras. Then John Cameron Mitchell walked in.

"OK, let's have you—" He pointed to "Keith," a burly, conventionally handsome LA guy who in his video had sat naked in front of a huge American flag and narrated a kidnapping fantasy come true. "—and you." He pointed to me.

Keith and I followed the director down the hall and into a small room where two cameras were trained on a somewhat battered gray love seat.

We sat down and John gave us our first scenario. "You're in the waiting room out there," he said, "and you've just watched the audition videos. And you know that once you're called into the room, you're going to have to kiss."

The conversation started off woodenly as we compared notes on the videos and gave each other our vital stats. "How old are you?" he asked. "Thirty-two," I answered. "What about you?" "Oh, I'm thirty-six," he said. "I'm really old."

"Well at least you're not as old as *John*," I said. "I think he's, like, thirty-nine."

My left ear curled, listening for a laugh from the director, and encountered silence.

My second audition was with the only other San Franciscan candidate, a boy in his mid-twenties named Jarrad whom I've kissed at a few parties and clubs back home. Jarrad, whose alter ego Suppositori Spelling is the reigning Miss Trannyshack, has no recollection of those encounters, but, acknowledging some alcohol-induced memory loss, doesn't categorically deny they took place.

After Jarrad and I had performed the same initial exercise, discussing the tapes and our upcoming audition, John pulled me out into the hallway to give me my instructions for the next scene. The premise was that I was calling up a phone sex line to enact a rape fantasy—that is, that I wanted to be raped. Jarrad, playing the phone sex operator, was given his own instructions out of my earshot.

I started off trying to take this one seriously. I adopted all the poses of low status—eyes downcast, toes pointed inward, brow furrowed—and with great pathos tried to convey the message, without spelling it out, that I wanted the phone sex operator also known as Suppositori Spelling to take me against my will.

As if that wasn't a steep enough challenge, Jarrad had suddenly become the improv partner from hell. He blocked me at every turn. Every offer I made, he dismissed; the best I could get from him was indifference. He was only following directions, it turned out—his assignment was to be a phone sex operator at the end of a long day, who's bored with his job in general and anxious to finish up with this call in particular.

"You're trying to humiliate me, aren't you?" I asked, after Jarrad roughly blocked me for the fifth time in a minute.

"Yeah, what *ever,*" he replied.

"It's OK—I deserve to be humiliated." Then I let my eyes go out of focus into the distance and declared solemnly: "I have low self-esteem."

The director howled with laughter.

Before leaving the office, I was assigned my first date—with Jarrad. I suggested that the two of us meet for drinks at 7:30. An hour later, waiting for Jarrad to show up, I found myself struggling to justify some of the audition week activities, particularly the hazily defined liaison Jarrad and I had been assigned.

Shortly before ten P.M., my phone started vibrating in my pants pocket. JOHN CAMERON MITCHELL read the LCD. I had left him a message earlier, when Jarrad first showed up, to ask him exactly what it was that we were supposed to be doing on this date. "Oh, it's no big deal. Just get to know one another, see what the chemistry is like," he'd said.

I told John I thought the date with Jarrad was going well and asked him how his day had been.

"Exhausting," he said. "But good. People were coming up

with really deep, personal material in the auditions today. It was kind of overwhelming."

Deep, personal material? Overwhelmingly exhausting deep personal material? I scanned quickly over my auditions: A flat joke about John's age. A rape fantasy with an uninterested rapist. Meanwhile the others had sat on that dingy love seat unpacking their souls and overwhelming him with pathos. *This is fun, this is fun, this is fun,* I had insisted all morning and into the afternoon. Perhaps I should have had a little less fun.

I was still preoccupied with what John had said about the afternoon's auditions and quickly set about dulling that anxiety at the open bar of a club in the East Village where a number of Sex Film Project dates were ending up. In addition to our colleagues, several of New York's most illustrious cross-dressers were there. After an hour or so I found myself crowded into a photo booth with a few others, including the legendary Justin Bond—a great performer and a genuine pseudocelebrity—as a little dime bag of cocaine made its way around. I was busy passing the bag when I felt my black cotton pants being yanked down and saw Justin Bond, seated on the photo booth stool, closing in on the kill.

I quickly fell to a squatting position, putting my genitals out of reach and bringing me face-to-knees with the drag diva.

"Justin, I swear to God, there's no way I would ever turn down a blow job from you except for the fact that I'm dating this guy—"

"I was just blotting my lipstick!" Justin interrupted me with nasal indignation. With that, she gathered her skirts with great dignity and sailed out of the photo booth.

I suppose I was asking for it, wearing those summery cotton pants with no underwear. A wide range of other hands, most of them attached to Sex Film Project candidates, had found their way underneath them already that night, including those of the burly, handsome Keith, whom I spent some time kissing next to the photo booth, and Jarrad, and two or three or four guys who were hanging around Jarrad. After two or three hours, the combination of the loose pants and loose guys playing in them resulted in the worst case of blue balls I've ever had in my life.

At around three in the morning, with Jarrad, I limped in acute pain back to the East Village apartment of a new friend of his, someone so well connected he was going to be in the Sex Film without even having to audition. I wasn't nearly drunk enough not to feel guilty about heading back to an East Village apartment with a Sex Film cast member and candidate, but in a number of conversations with the boyfriend that day I had come to what I thought was a practical compromise to govern my sexual behavior for the week. So I explained to Jarrad that I was in a relationship with a really amazing guy at home, and that while he was tolerating this week and this date, I would have to rein it in on our date tonight: kissing and jerking off were my limits.

"I'm going to hold you to that," Jarrad whispered to me as we entered his new friend's tiny fourth-floor walk-up. I appreciated the sentiment, but it was entirely academic, because all I was capable of doing for the first twenty minutes while Jarrad and his friend went at it next to me on the bed was to hold a refrigerated bottle of Rolling Rock to my aching testicles, which were swollen to the size of Meyer lemons. Once the swelling went down and the beer was at room temperature, I jerked off, coming on Jarrad, his new friend, and his new friend's ceiling. Then I gathered my things, kissed my date good-bye, and walked through the crisp spring dawn back to TriBeCa.

Saturday, after waking late in the afternoon, I spent the remaining daylight and early evening hours writing in this diary. Then I set out for the East Village, where I was assigned to meet, for a date, a dirty-blond, tanned guy about my age who knew the parent doppelgängers portrayed in my audition video. I was late meeting him at the Wonder Bar on East 6th Street, and worried that this had something to do with the fact that he seemed approximately as enthusiastic about being on a date with me as, say, fishing cigarette butts out of the East River with a tea strainer.

"How'd your date go?" a friend asked me when it was over.

"He talked about himself for forty minutes," I reported.

"Hot!" the friend said. It was now about eleven o'clock, and the narrow bar had filled up with Sex Film candidates and other loose characters. Auditions continued on Sunday, but this gathering in the Wonder Bar was in essence the closing ceremonies, the last official Sex Film activity for this group. For that reason, and because a number of us had seen the sun rise in unfamiliar neighborhoods that morning, the mood was several shades darker than it had been the night before; in addition to being hungover, we were starting to get paranoid. We were making calculations, weighing rumors, sizing up the competition, wondering darkly about that guy who used to be on *3rd Rock from the Sun*, counting up the number of auditions and dates we were called for, trying to divine our respective futures from everything John said and the way he said it and how it compared with what he had said to the others.

My friends among the candidates were confident of their failure. Keith hadn't been asked to audition again and was sure he'd been eliminated. Jarrad had another audition scheduled, but no date. I, by contrast, felt pretty good about being two and two for dates and auditions—I had been called to appear again at noon the next day. Then, at the Wonder Bar, a guy told me he'd been called to audition all three days, had had two dates, and had been interviewed in private by HBO for their documentary about the auditions. Into this schedule I read my doom.

No longer were we all one big happy family working in concert toward some bold and noble goal of artistic and sexual liberty. Now we were thirty-four dirty-minded siblings competing for the attention and love of a single parent who was unfailingly affectionate but neglectful by virtue of his miraculous potency, charisma, and popularity. The dinner hour was upon us, and the competition for the four or five servings of John's stew of art, achievement, and notoriety was now as acute as our hunger for them.

I'd underestimated the seriousness of this whole venture until now. I had fallen for John's ruse, had let him lull me into thinking this was sex therapy improv camp instead of an audition that would determine the course of the rest of my career and the rest of my life. He had lulled us, sitting in that theater at the Archives, into thinking that we were embarking on this daring adventure together, when of course most of us would be left behind. The drug of his presence and charisma was starting to wear off, and the reality of the audition, of the rejection and disappointment that were inevitably in store for most of us, was starting to hurt. As I sidled through the crowded bar, all I could remember from the week were the idiotic things that had come out of my mouth, the sentences in this diary I cringed to think he'd read. The cycle is familiar because it is so much like love, or the phase of it in which we contemplate the possibility that we are no longer loved in return. We did not come to New York to date each other; we came to New York to date John. Now we waited by the phone.

Having been shaken off by my date, the self-involved dirty blond, I milled around, making conversation with the other candidates. The flow of available small talk quickly grew infinitesimal before running completely dry. The awkwardness was keenest with the other gay guys: the most direct competition and, I increasingly thought, the most vulnerable. Throughout the week the project had produced a kind of gay superiority complex, in which we fags were chummy with John and with each other and enjoyed, if not flaunted, our majority status and our instinctual, gay-given comfort with the whole idea of fucking strangers on the one hand and fucking on film on the other.

The illusion that this majority status benefited us was one of Saturday night's first casualties. In my conversation with John at his apartment, he had mentioned female ejaculation at least twice and said how he was becoming more and more interested in having the movie explore female sexuality. How many women, and straight men to fuck them, did the candidate pool offer John to choose from? At best a handful. Now, at the Wonder Bar's closing ceremonies, I started envying heterosexual odds. Transgendered odds wouldn't be bad either. If the cast list didn't include the young blond hooker whose midvideo sex switch had mind-fucked even this gender-jaded group, I'd eat my chromosomes.

Milling around the Wonder Bar, all my gay male comrades could talk about was casting anxiety. I had a fairly long talk with "Plato," a guy I'd met one night about a year before along with several other skinny white twentysomething chem-friendly photographers, circus performers, hookers, and drug dealers at the Los Angeles mansion of an art- and artist-collecting corporate lawyer. I'd been instantly attracted to Plato, not least because, in addition to having those smoldering rent-boy good looks, he was a writer. At the Wonder Bar we commiserated for a while about the psychic brutalities of writing, and then about the building anxiety of the week's audition process.

Plato's anxiety, it turned out, was more severe than my own.

One of the other candidates was his boyfriend, which offered two distinctly horrifying scenarios in which one would be cast and not the other. And then there was Plato's long-standing friendship with John, which had already weathered the director's decision, after Plato had given what all agreed was the best audition of his life, to cast someone a little younger as Tommy Gnosis in the *Hedwig* movie. How would the friendship weather another disappointment at John's hands? How did that consideration affect the chances of the rest of us? What must John be going through, weighing friendships with people he'd disappointed before, matching sexual orientations and chemistries between close friends on the one hand and people he'd never met on the other, between people who live in this atmosphere and others like me who were giddy with the novelty of it?

I was preparing to leave the Wonder Bar when Jarrad arrived, so resplendent in Suppositori Spelling drag that no one recognized him. His powder-blue knee-high fuck-me pumps added at least six inches to his height, and the makeup and colorless Wonder Woman armored top and bikini underpants with no tuck completed the metamorphosis. I was relieved to see him, then dismayed, as it became apparent that the bond we'd formed had succumbed to the oddsmaking calculation and anxiety that had poisoned the rest of the candidate pool. Jarrad fretted. Why hadn't John assigned him a date? I shrugged my shoulders. Our subsequent small talk could have fit comfortably into a dime bag.

At a loss for words, I looked around and saw the back of a head of spiky brown and white-pepper hair on a petite frame: John. I resolved to avoid him—any interaction with the director in this crushing atmosphere could only result in misbehavior, foot-in-mouth outbreaks, and regret. A minute later the crowd had shifted so that he was right in front of me, the nape of his pale neck exposed and beckoning to me in the obscurity of the bar like a spinning aluminum lure in a murky pond. That skin seemed so naked, so inviting, so vulnerable, that my resolution to avoid John transformed into a considerably more powerful desire to kiss him, and before I could think through my actions, my lips were feeling the warmth of his neck and my tongue tasting the salt of his skin as I sucked lightly, came up for air, then kissed the spot once more.

John turned around, inquisitive but not necessarily surprised, then smiled broadly as he recognized me. He backed into me and drew my arm forward around him so that we were spooning standing up, then ground his bottom into my groin in time to the music, all the while maintaining his conversation with a woman I didn't recognize. He bummed a puff of her cigarette, and I squeezed him to give me one too. He didn't get it at first, until I said, into his ear, "Hook me up." Was that pushy? He held the cigarette to my mouth and I drew in smoke, exhaled, and released him.

Walking home from the Wonder Bar, I heard something rustling in a garbage can, freshly lined with a blue plastic bag. I stood before it awhile, contemplating the hours of hunger and thirst it would take for that bag to become still. Then I did something I can only confess now that I am three thousand miles from New York and New Yorkers: I removed the liner and liberated a small rat, which scurried into the dark recesses of the West Village to scavenge and breed.

John called me in to audition with Plato. This was good news—I wanted to go dark, and Plato was so dark he dimmed any room he entered. John held me in the hallway while he sent Plato to the love seat.

"OK, the deal is that you're calling a sex line—" Fuck me. "—and what you want this guy to do is reenact an ideal sexual scenario you always have in your mind, a sexual touchstone for you. And the scenario could be real or imagined."

Before he'd finished saying this into my ear I had my image. It was of the hermaphrodite in Fellini's *Satyricon*. I saw this beautiful young person (not, perhaps, as illegally young as Fellini portrayed him) lying naked, exposing his pale breasts and body and micropenis, pubic hair transformed into a white froth in the refulgent summer sun on a wide slab of granite in the Yuba River where it flows through the Sierra foothills and where I spent three days one summer without leaving. I barely moved from that rock in those three days, and that's how I envisioned the scenario with the hermaphrodite, willfully stranded in this exalted aerie, thirty feet above a diving pool in the river. Only a glimpse of this image came to me in that moment, accompanied by the beats of pipe-organ dissonances shimmering in the air like heat rising from the rock, but it told me down to the last detail everything I had to say and do for the next twenty minutes.

Oh, it started off veering toward farce, just like the others—I repeatedly had to ask Plato to make his deep voice higher, and I wound up talking dirty to him about his "little clit of a dick." This made the director laugh out loud, as Plato is famed across nine time zones for being distinctly not little. But from hormone and dick jokes Plato's gravity pulled us down, and at that lower altitude I was able to say a number of very involved things about the way loving him had made me feel whole, because his manifest conflict between sexes reflected the less visible conflicts within my own identity—between ways of being, self-presentation, even my passionate (not necessarily sexual) orientations. We shared the experience of feeling "neither here nor there." I barely remember a line of the dialogue now, only this resonant memory of what it was like to feel that the words coming out of my mouth to describe my longing for this person who once loved me were having a palpable effect on the temperature and atmospheric pressure of the room.

Plato was right there with me, and I with him, feigning this heartbreak while he pretended to be the sex worker pretending to be a hermaphrodite. The dialogue went on for a long time. At Plato's perfectly timed cue, it got dirty. Then it became sad, and I began to suspect, without saying anything about it, that the reason I missed the hermaphrodite was that the hermaphrodite was dead. Plato said something to buck me up, and I smiled painfully through an upwelling of tears. When it was over, there was a good fifteen seconds of silence. Finally, John spoke, in a husky voice, blinking back tears of his own. "That's what this movie has to be about," he said. "Because that person could be anybody."

I looked at John, as did Plato. I didn't blink or alter my expression. John said a few more things about the audition, ordered an improv hug between Plato and me, and then dismissed the two of us for the day.

The following Monday, I flew back to San Francisco. I was not home two days before I ran into a friend—a documentary filmmaker and friend of John's for many years—who welcomed me back and asked cheerfully how the audition went. Oh, and had I heard? The movie was cast. There were only four leads. One of them was Jarrad, another was that guy from *3rd Rock from the Sun*. But the information was fifth-hand, he added, so I should take it with a grain of salt.

If there's one thing three years at the Juilliard School trained me to do, it is to smile and continue a conversation amicably after having had the wind knocked out of me by disappointment, and this is what I did with the documentary filmmaker.

That night, I lay in bed in an agitated wakefulness that exhausted not only me but my boyfriend, who had given me an ecstatic welcome home and now lay beside me, awake, as I tossed and turned. I found myself in the difficult position of begging solace not only from someone who was immensely relieved by the news that had hurt me, but from someone whom I had spent that matchless week in New York hurting.

Still, I confided in him, and he listened and did his best to comfort me. Some of his responses stung, though, as he held up a mirror before my feelings of rejection and envy. I confessed to him that as much as I wanted to be happy for Jarrad, all I could think was how difficult it would be to hear him talk about the month-long improv workshop, about John this and John that, about the shooting schedule, the parties, the premiere.

"That's exactly how I would have felt if you'd been cast," my boyfriend said matter-of-factly.

Near dawn, I got out of bed and brought my computer to the hallway, where I e-mailed John. If my sources had it right, I wrote, I wouldn't be coming back east for the workshop, and so I wanted to thank him for inviting me to one of the strangest and most wonderful challenges—certainly among those filed under "audition"—of my life.

Then I slept. When I woke up a few hours later there was a reply in my inbox: "Paul, I don't know who your sources are but I AM leaning towards different people right now—partly because they are in relationships already (those things are a big deal as I discovered and you know). But absolutely nothing is for sure right now. I'm truly right in the middle of it all. Which is not to take away from how wonderful you were. Your improv about your intersex friend on the rock almost killed me it was so beautiful. Thank you so much and we'll talk. Love, JCM."

First I felt that kick in the gut again—of course I was hoping he would refute the rumor entirely. Then I naturally enough took the intended solace in his praise, which on second glance brought me a new rush of pride. *Your improv about your intersex friend on the rock.* The director hadn't merely found it beautiful, he had bought it. With some stolen help from Fellini, from the transgendered blond Sex Film candidate, from those luminous bars of remembered organ music, even from John Updike (whose hooker in *Rabbit, Run* had a "brass froth" of pubic hair), and aided by Plato's openness and immediacy, I had spontaneously written and performed a fiction and passed it off as memory. If only for a twenty-minute audition, I'd surpassed my most grandiose fantasies about this venture. I did not leave New York a celebrity, pseudo or otherwise; I didn't even leave with a part. But for those twenty minutes of sex and pathos on that battered love seat next to Plato, I was an actor.

The days went by, the sting of rejection dulled, and the final cast list came out. (Plato and his boyfriend, the transgendered hooker and the boy who fucked his bleeding girlfriend, the guy who had three audition calls, two dates, and a private interview with HBO, the Chinese-Canadian woman who had played Korean in the *Hedwig* movie, the guy who sent in an audition tape because he was "a complete whore" and a few more for good measure, but not Jarrad and not that guy from *3rd Rock from the Sun.*) I couldn't help thinking about another homosexual ingenue from the provinces who came to New York hoping to rise to stardom on the stage with the help of her forty-year-old idol.

Wasn't I a slightly less evil twenty-first-century version of Eve Harrington? I'll grant that the antiheroine of *All About Eve* plotted her course with malice and subterfuge, and that she, unlike me, completed it successfully. But both of us sat on a couch on Broadway and told our idol a startlingly sad story of love lost, made that idol cry, and made that idol believe our lies.

And though Eve fed off souls greater than her own for the sake of her career and artistry, while I merely held out my hand for that nourishment in earnestness and hope, we shared a dangerous instability. Both of us were searching for an identity we could not manifest on our own, but had to have conferred: by our respective mentors, by the stage, by fame. Both of us were a fraud, or felt like one, skilled at imitation, a personal palimpsest onto which any character or effect could be written.

Initially, I wondered whether this audition would expose me, my fraudulence, my incapacity to act truly under the imaginary circumstances of the play or in the reality of my own life. Or would they discover me—see me for who I really was and make me a star?

"Honey, there's a step in between, which is 'I accept myself as a real person,' " a close friend told me in response to all of this. I did, and I do, on some level. But there is something in me, the part of me hung up on celebrity and John's praise, the part of me crushed by his rejection, that does not accept the reality of who I am.

The theatrical fable of Eve Harrington's encounter with the great Margo Channing is told as a lesbian vampire story, the younger actress sucking the creative and erotic life out of her mentor. The passionate feelings I felt for John were real—but they were also inextricable from the work he did and the gifts he could have chosen to bestow on me. As a lifelong collector of mentors, of substitute parents—whether movie directors or musical pedagogues or swinging bisexual couples, all of whom I feel compelled to write about in public and in intimate detail—I both hate this conflict of motive and passion and accept it as the inevitable consequence of being called. As for the pleasures and hazards of being chosen—those are once more deferred.

Man-Hunting with the High-School Dream Girls
David Amsden

One in the morning! Tonight is tomorrow, and disbelief is suspended—or at least left outside on the curb, blocked by the velvet rope. Inside a vaguely South African–themed nightclub called Cain, a pale-skinned, blonde-haired girl named Sophie is on the dance floor. She sports a yellow blouse with a plunging neckline, white jeans that look grafted to her skin, and shimmery ice-pick heels. Yesterday, Sophie graduated from a certain all-girls private school uptown, and she is still three years shy of being legal in such an establishment, though right now that's irrelevant. Right now, Sophie is a woman in her twenties, just like her ID says, and just like she told the guy in the preppie blazer with the gelled-back hair on the dance floor. He's sort of annoying. But sort of cute too. And very likely graduated from high school right around the time Sophie was born.

"Him? Yeah, I think he's, like, thirty-five, or even forty," observes Sophie's friend Audrey. "She hooked up with him last week at Lotus."

Audrey is also eighteen, also pale and blonde. When she imagines herself in ten years she sees a successful woman working as "a representative of some corporation. Like if I'm doing press for JPMorgan, that's fine." She is slouched in the banquette running alongside the dance floor, sipping her second Grey Goose and cranberry. Next to her is Lana, seventeen, all long brown hair and big, drowsy brown eyes. The three girls (whose names have been changed "because otherwise our parents will freak") are jaunty, sweet-natured, sophisticated, and acutely self-aware. They know which is the dessert fork. The last time any of them looked their age, they were in elementary school. Like so many privileged New York kids, they have been taught, since they were small children, never to act like children.

"*Apparently* I hooked up with him last week at Lotus, but I don't remember" is how Sophie had described the incident to her friends earlier that day over lunch at Nello, on Madison Avenue. "That was totally uncharacteristic, and you know it. I don't just randomly hook up with people. I can count the number of guys I've *kissed* on—" Sophie did some math with her manicured fingers. "—two hands. But I'd only had a sushi roll for dinner, and we drank way too much."

Audrey rolled her eyes and mentioned another guy from the Lotus night, a man who was married.

Sophie: "I didn't hook up with him!"

Audrey: "Oh, I thought you did."

"The married guy kissed me, but we didn't hook up," Sophie clarified. At that, the girls cracked up.

Such is the secret life of a certain kind of New York girl: precocious, a touch lonely, alienated by boys her age, and eager to trade in the husk of adolescence for the façade of womanhood by spending a few nights a week in places she's technically not allowed to go. If not Cain, then Marquee; if not Marquee, then PM; if not PM, then Bungalow 8; if not Bungalow 8, then Hiro. The lighting is dim, the music loud. Reality chips apart. Assistants become partners at the firm, married men are temporarily single, fifth-floor walk-ups morph into luxury lofts, and high school girls become the most eligible women in the room. Being a teenager anywhere is to want, more than anything, to be *old*; being a teenager in the ageless playground of New York City—especially a girl, especially at night—is to be able to pull it off. And in this age of perpetual adolescence, when adults worship teenage pop deities like Lindsay Lohan—whom Audrey saw the other night in the bathroom at Bungalow 8—there are plenty of men with receding hairlines and disposable incomes who want to play twenty-one, too.

"But it's complicated," Sophie explained as the waiter cleared her pasta at Nello. "It's nice going out and meeting older guys, but at the same time it's also kind of weird." Until recently, Sophie was dating a guy in his twenties who lived with an older married couple in the luxury-magazine business. She'd lie to her parents ("Mom, I'm crashing at Audrey's...") only to find herself accidentally emulating her parents' lifestyle. "It was like I was hanging out with who my parents were ten years ago," she said. "But that's nothing. Did you guys hear about—?" Sophie whispered the name of a classmate. "She was sleeping with this married guy in his forties. He had *kids*. That is just wrong."

"Ewww, are you serious?" asked Lana.

Stories like these hover about. The girl involved with the music exec, the girl who had an affair with a Hamptons promoter, the girl who found herself skinny-dipping in a rooftop pool with some gray-haired guy. Even Audrey recently went to dinner with a lawyer the girls pegged at about forty-five years old. He told her that "he got a lot of free stuff," invitations to private parties, movie premieres, sample sales, sneak peeks, you name it—and that she and her friends were welcome to come along anytime. It was the standard older-guy pitch. Audrey went because she wanted to see, as she put it, "if he just wanted to be friends or what." They went to Nello.

"People were giving him weird looks," said Audrey, summing up the night for Sophie and Lana. "I felt awkward. He was just really underdressed. I was considering going out with him, but not the way he was dressed. In the end he paid for dinner and I had a really good meal. I had fifty-dollar ravioli."

"I feel bad using guys," said Lana. "I feel like there's always an obligation."

"Yeah, Audrey," Sophie chimed in. "What are you doing?"

"I don't know!" cried Audrey. "I've never done this with any man. It's just…" She paused. "At least he's not a seventeen-year-old boy, you know?"

"I know," agreed Lana. "I have nothing to say to those boys."

"I honestly feel like a thirty-year-old trapped in the body of a high-school girl," said Audrey. "I don't know if that goes for all girls in New York, or just us, if it's just the life we've been living."

It's like when they watch *Sex and the City*: What they see is not the story of four women twice their age looking for genuine love in superficial surroundings. They see themselves.

"I'm ready, honestly, to be married and pregnant," said Lana. "Not children, but just pregnant. I know how it sounds. I don't care. I want to have my belly and my man."

"Me too," said Audrey. "People say I should be excited about college, but I'm like, 'Um, no.' I want to get on with my life." She sipped her iced tea and added, "I've never been in love."

"Me neither," said Lana quietly. "We're going to be single all our lives." They considered this.

"What are we doing later?"

"As far as the girls go, here's how it works," says Richard Sung, aka DJ Crooked, perched in the DJ booth at a vaguely Japanese-themed club called Hiro, one of the girls' favorite spots to dance. It's a typical Thursday night, packed and palpitating; a woman wearing spandex lingerie swings gracefully from the ceiling. A regular at such places, Sung has developed a philosophy about the subtext of New York nightlife: "The more upscale the club, the younger the girls and older the guys. Look around. The girls out there, they're anywhere between eighteen and, maximum, twenty-three. The guys are twenty-three to, like, fifty. It's why it works, you know? It's fucked up, but whatever."

The girls decide that Hiro isn't happening tonight, and head over to Gypsy Tea, a club on 24th Street that feels a lot like Hiro. They sit at the owner's table and dance on the dark couches. Around them, like a halo, stands a ring of older men staring, hoping, debating first lines in their minds. "My feeling is that if they're in here, they're twenty-one," says a ruddy-faced man in his forties with a crew cut. "And that's where I stop asking questions. So you can tell me they're eighteen and I'm basically just like, 'Shut the fuck up.' "

A thirtyish guy with slicked-back hair in a pink polo shirt approaches Lana, sticks out his fleshy hand, and says, "Dance with me." A moment later she is sandwiched between him and his friend, who's wearing a blue polo shirt. Eventually, Sophie and

Audrey pull Lana away. The polo pals high-five each other.

Pink shirt: "I'm just here to get laid."

Blue shirt: "But it never happens with little girls like that."

Overhearing this, a thirty-one-year-old guy wearing a black suit and baseball cap shakes his head. "It kind of disturbs me to see all my friends hitting on girls twenty years younger than them," he says. "I guess the girls just don't care. Maybe they just care about the money, I don't know. It all comes down to that because, come on, it's not like they're going to *fall in love* in a place like this. They can't possibly think they will. I'll tell you, I feel really terrible for women my age, in their thirties and forties. There's no market for them anymore. Everything is about girls like these." He takes a sip of his Heineken and suddenly changes his tone. "But, God, they're the hottest people in here, aren't they?"

Tonight at Cain, the girls have a "table," meaning they've agreed to spend six hundred dollars for the minimum two bottles of liquor, which in turn gives them a sliver of prime real estate on the banquette. "Look, a place like this is all about money first," explains Adam Alpert, a promoter for Cain who is standing next to the DJ as the girls stroll inside. "First money, then celebs, then the girls, who are really just here to feel cool and meet older guys with money."

No one has discussed who is going to pay for the bottles tonight. When Sophie was hanging out with the married couple, the husband tended to pay, but ever since that relationship sputtered out, she and her friends have scrounged together cash from their allowances. They don't pay with credit cards, because at clubs like this, you have to show ID when using a credit card, and the moment you do that is the moment the artifice crumbles.

The girls are dancing to House of Pain's "Jump Around," a song almost older than they are, when one of the DJs makes his way over to Lana. Outside of clubs, Lana is shy, even a little clumsy.

She looks younger than the other girls, although that didn't stop a twenty-seven-year-old from asking her out on her fifteenth birthday. "I wouldn't have been into the whole going-out thing if it weren't for them," she says of Sophie and Audrey. More than club life, Lana likes sleeping over at Audrey's apartment, staying up all night listening to Stevie Wonder and mocking Audrey's taste in corny movies. But inside a club, something shifts and Lana becomes one of those dancers who are disturbingly confident. She stretches out her arms, leans back, shakes her shoulders—"That's her move," says Sophie—and the men jockey for position. The DJ is a hell of a dancer—handsome, too, in a personal-trainer sort of way—and probably somewhere around twenty-five. It's an age Lana has developed a theory about. "It's like the whole quarter-life-crisis thing," she likes to say. "Guys in their twenties, they feel like they're getting older. They're starting to look back. So they come to us, wanting to feel a little younger, a little more free-spirited and lighthearted."

In theory, anyway. The reality is more complicated. Lana recently had a bad experience with a guy that age. It all went down at the prom, of all places, the whole debacle an unfortunate reminder of the pitfalls of growing up in a city where no one acts their age. Three weeks ago, the girls made what in retrospect proved to be a poor decision: asking some twentysomething finance guys they were seeing to be their prom dates. The guys did everything they could to get out of it. They didn't have tuxedos, they said. Didn't know where to buy corsages. One even confessed that he was being seriously chastised by his friends. And so the girls did everything they could to ease the discomfort: paying for a private table, renting an Expedition instead of sharing a limo with their classmates. But the illusion was already infected by reality, and the night was a disaster.

"It wasn't a good idea to bring them there," says Audrey. "It just made everything too concrete, the fact that we are still in high school."

It was Lana's date who had the crisis of conscience. He left in the middle of the dance. That he and Lana had been sleeping together for a few weeks made this all the more intense. Lana thought everything was going to work out when they met up after the prom at PM and she found herself on the dance floor with her boyfriend. He was kissing her neck and whispering in her ear, "You're so sweet, you're adorable, you're perfect, and, you know, we have really great conversations. Really, you're everything I want." For a moment, Lana thought he was simply apologizing for acting like such a child at the prom and started kissing him back. That's when he said it, the part about not being sure it was going to work between them.

"You know," she tried, "I don't expect anything from you."

Then he said something that's been ringing in her ears ever since: "But whenever we do stuff, I just feel guilty about it afterward."

Guilty! He'd just pawned off his shame on her! How...*juvenile!*

Lana ran outside to the Expedition and had a drink in the backseat. It was 5:30 in the morning. She wanted to go home, but just then a limo pulled up next to her car—a limo that had nothing to do with the prom. Things were blurry. Somehow Lana and a friend ended up in the limo. Just dumped by a guy in his twenties, now she was riding around with a bunch of "Eurotrash guys in their forties and fifties." One of the men put a dollar bill in her purse that turned out to be filled with cocaine. Another did a line off her friend's hand. Lana doesn't do coke—none of her friends do; they've seen too many of their classmates go through rehab—and couldn't figure out if what was happening was comic or tragic.

When everyone started talking about going back to the hotel, "to party," Lana hailed a cab.

"That night was crazy," she recalls, without a trace of nostalgia. The truth was, dumb as it sounds, she'd just wanted a normal prom night. She wanted to feel, for once, before she was no longer a teenage girl, *like* a teenage girl. "Sometimes I hate this city," she says. "Sometimes I hate what growing up here does to you."

All night long at Cain, the men come and go, buying drinks, paying compliments, attempting to dance, asking for numbers. The guy in the preppie blazer whom Sophie hooked up with at Lotus comes over for one more attempt, suggesting they all get a drink sometime soon—like maybe in the next hour, maybe someplace quiet. When it's clear that he's not going to get a repeat performance, he finally says good-bye.

As the crowd thins, the bill arrives: nine hundred dollars. "What the fuck is this?" demands Audrey. Apparently someone ordered a third bottle, which has barely been touched. The girls had hoped that the college boys in their entourage might pay for the liquor, but they're refusing. And the girls have only two hundred dollars in cash. "We will call the police," the manager says sternly, ignoring the fact that if the police are called, it's the club that will be in real trouble. Audrey thinks about those nights out with the married guy, the one Sophie's ex-boyfriend lived with, how men like that always paid and generally treated the girls with chivalry, like grown-ups. For now though, she'll have to be a grown-up, sort of, and take care of things herself. She makes cute faces, professes ignorance, apologizes. Eventually, her antics get the third bottle removed from their bill. In the meantime, Lana and Sophie are over it. They yawn dramatically, leave their money with Audrey, and head outside.

"Whatever," says Sophie. "I'm tired."

"I'll call you tomorrow," says Lana. "We should go out."
"For sure."
Kiss-kiss. And good-night.

The Pole Test

Natalie Y. Moore &
Natalie Hopkinson

I look into my daughter's eyes
And realize that I'ma learn through her.

—Common, "Be"

Comedian Chris Rock prowls the stage, bright lights blazing around him, his mouth running at a clip. He cuts an impressive figure in his black-and-wine-colored striped suit as he surveys the audience at historic Constitution Hall in Washington, D.C. He's taping an HBO stand-up special called *Never Scared*, but as soon as the talk turns to fatherhood, it's clear that the man is *shook*. Black male comedians have given us a variety of takes on black fatherhood. There are the late Robin Harris, Bernie Mac, D. L. Hughley, who describe the anguish of fathering bad-ass kids, also known as "Bebe." Others, like Cosby and Murphy, play the role of sober moralists.

Chris Rock takes the high road when the talk turns to his beloved baby girl. Worry lines crease his face, his visage full of angst. His eyes, always wild, appear to flash with genuine fear. He worries aloud how what he does now will shape his daughter's future relationships. He does not want to send yet another woman out into the dating world with "daddy issues." After much thought and consideration, Rock says he's figured out his responsibility as a father to a little girl.

"My only job in life is to keep her off the pole," Rock says soberly. "They don't grade fathers, but if your daughter's a stripper, you fucked up!"

The idiom of fathers, daughters, and the stripper's pole has pierced black lexicon like memorable lines from *Def Comedy Jam* or *In Living Color*. By Rock's estimation, a whole lot of men are fucking up in America. Somebody produced the sperm that spawned all those booties grinding on BET's soft-porn video show *Uncut*. Someone helped populate the cult-hit documentaries *Pimps Up Ho's Down* and *American Pimp*. Someone sired the stripper-turned-emcee-turned-fashion-star Eve. What rapper hasn't included rhymes about strippers, from Ludacris to the Ying Yang Twins to the Notorious B.I.G.? A crop of books dubbed "hip-hop literature" is following the tradition of 1970s paperback blaxploitation writers Iceberg Slim and Donald Goines, whose books are filled with hustlers and strippers.

And someone birthed hip-hop, whose entire aesthetic—at least as promulgated on cable and radio—seems to be based on the world's oldest profession; all men are P-I-M-P-S and all the women are hos. As a whole, the hip-hop generation has found prostitution to be an apt metaphor for American capitalism, which under our generation's watch has taken the literal and figurative pimping of black culture to new depths.

But Rock isn't just speaking in metaphors before the sold-out Constitution Hall audience. The grip that strippers hold over men is as real as it gets. It can be a force as strong as heroin, as the married Chris Rock personally attests. "Someone has got to entertain the married men of America," he says. This is not to disparage the strippers, Rock says. He means them no offense, he says over and over again. "Somebody's got to do it," he says, shrugging.

So this is how a new standard for black fatherhood has been set; call it the "pole test." Judging by the number of times keeping his daughter off the pole has been repeated, like most great comedy it taps into a deeper kind of truth. To us, it begs the question: But seriously, who *are* these men? Don't look to popular culture for answers. Strippers are almost never allotted a high degree of character development, whether before the camera or on the stage. To get answers, you've got to ask the strippers themselves.

We asked four strippers, all randomly selected through personal contacts—one on the East Coast, one on the West, and two in between—about their relationships with their dads. These are four women, four different paths. Our sampling, by the way, says nothing empirical about how contemporary black men father their girls. As a symbol of patriarchy, though, the stories of these women say a whole lot. We'll leave the psychoanalysis to the professionals. But listen closely and you'll hear the many ways that the porn industry, and the Married Men of America filling the audience, have fathered these women, providing a near lifetime of guidance, affirmation, and sustenance. Both biologically and figuratively, the answer to the question "Who's your daddy?" is complicated. These women are reluctant to assign blame. They protect their daddies, whether familiar, monstrous, or strange, as fiercely as they protect themselves.

Yasmine dances at a strip club on Michigan Avenue in Detroit. Men in athletic jerseys, men in suits inhale steak specials and topless women on poles. Women are not allowed inside unless they are employees or arrive with a male escort. Fluorescent lights flicker inside, and on the sunniest day the club is midnight-dark.

The bubblegum-pink dressing room is small. Mindless chatter bounces off the walls, the kind heard in a high school girls' locker room. The twentysomething dancers click-clack in the classic clear heels that Chris Rock dubs the official "ho uniform." A television rests atop a vending machine peddling eight-dollar cigarettes. In the background, sounds of suburban domesticity waft from an *Everybody Loves Raymond* episode, followed by the catfights on the catwalks on *America's Next Top Model*.

Inside, flesh is everywhere. Half-dressed dancers fasten each other's hooks and zippers, compare boob jobs, and flaunt goodies from their shopping excursions. The cell phones never seem to stop ringing. Hot curling irons line the horizontal mirror.

Yasmine enters. Cornrowed extensions fall down her back, fake hazel contacts stare at us from above exposed breasts. A tongue ring flashes when she speaks.

> *"Make the money, don't let it make you."*
> *"Closed legs don't get fed."*
> —from the film *The Players Club*

"I'm your daddy," said the tall, dark man with a receding hairline and thick Coke-bottle glasses pushed above his nose. Yasmine was eleven years old. All of her short life she thought her younger brother's father was hers. Plus, she had a stepfather at home. When her mother had a nervous breakdown, triggered by getting strung out on cocaine-laced weed, the five siblings were sent different ways. The summer day in 1991 when Yasmine moved in was the day she met the man.

She was not exactly impressed. Yasmine's mother had instructed her to refer to all her boyfriends as "Daddy."

Now Yasmine stared at the man claiming to be her biological father. "You and every other nigga," Yasmine recalls as her reply.

When she recounts this story, Yasmine is fresh from Cancún, her brown skin lightly sun-kissed. She has exchanged braids for a long, bouncy weave. She is still reeling from the news she learned earlier that day—that a childhood eye injury has grown into glaucoma. Before her steaming plate of lamb chops and buttery baked potato arrives, the bartender slides Yasmine a drink. A Purple Rain—a shot each of gin, rum, vodka, schnapps, Chambord, and triple sec—helps loosen her inhibitions and her tongue.

Yasmine struggled even before she moved into her father's house. As an eight-year-old, she assumed motherly duties, grocery shopping with five hundred dollars worth of food stamps lining her pockets. In sixth grade Yasmine would arrive at school hours before sunrise to escape her mentally unstable mother's home, often dressed in the same clothes as the day before. She had unbrushed teeth and rumpled hair. The child smelled ripe. Teachers never inquired about her problems, so Yasmine lost faith in them.

When Yasmine moved in with her biological father and his longtime girlfriend, their two daughters were part of the package. Her torture started soon afterward. Her father's girlfriend was happy to play the role of the evil stepmother, putting the tweener to work—and on birth control pills. Yasmine had developed a figure early, and her period debuted at age nine. Family gossip about a previous rape led them to believe that an early introduction to sex would surely lead to promiscuity.

One night before school resumed that fall, Yasmine sat on the floor, her back against her father's bed. His girlfriend snoozed under the covers. Her father forced his hand down Yasmine's shirt and massaged her 34C breasts. Then the rape started. It became a routine. After his girlfriend fell asleep he'd have sex with Yasmine, his eldest daughter.

"After a while I got used to it. I was used to disappointment. My mother let me down. Why did they send me to a father I didn't know? I didn't believe he was my fucking father."

If child protective services knocked on the door and questioned her about abuse, tipped off by the neighbors' suspicions, Yasmine lied. They said they wouldn't remove her from the home regardless of how she answered. "The system is a joke," Yasmine huffs.

Her dad fooled people by playing the role of an overprotective father. He insisted on attending her eighth-grade prom and would show up at school dances. When Yasmine resisted his sexual advances—he'd wake her up to meet him in the basement—a beat down was as inevitable as getting raped the next day. She found an outlet in writing letters to herself describing the abuse. Why cry, Yasmine thought. Alas, her father's girlfriend discovered the letters and passed them around to other family members like embarrassing school notes as they drank cocktails and ate crab legs. No one believed Yasmine. And Yasmine was nothing but a nasty bitch anyway, her quasi stepmother would shriek. Yasmine saw a psychologist after her mother's breakdown. The psychologist reported back to her father and his girlfriend that the teen made up the story about her father's abuse.

"How can I have sex with a grown-ass man?" she asked.

Yasmine ran away several times. She tired of being raped three or four times a week and being treated like a backwoods stepchild, time and again receiving paltry Christmas presents while her younger sisters rejoiced in a Toys "R" Us windfall. At fifteen she fled to stay with a good friend's aunt, who welcomed her. The woman moved to the South and longed to take Yasmine with her, but her father refused. Afterward, he and his live-in girlfriend broke up. Yasmine and her father moved into a new house. "I was hoping things would change. That's the worst thing that could've happened. It went from sugar to shit," she says.

His drinking escalated, and the two shared a bed. When she got pregnant, neighbors speculated that Yasmine carried his child. But this time no one intervened. And he could talk his way out of anything, often threatening to send her to a juvenile home. Thankfully, he was not the child's father. The sex finally stopped at age eighteen when Yasmine got pregnant again by another guy. When her father crept toward her in a sexual advance, Yasmine hit him. He pulled a gun on her. She moved out, physically unscathed, and emancipated herself.

She had to find a way to support herself. Working at the fast-food chain White Castle wasn't cutting it. Yasmine's cousin and her friends always sported new clothes, hairdos, and immaculate make-up. They stripped for a living. "I wanted to live like them," she recalls. She had graduated from high school on the honor roll and got accepted into a community college, but her father had belittled that idea when she lived under his watch, insisting school wasn't a place for a girl with kids. Instead she prepared for life as a stripper.

Living on her own, Yasmine tried to make amends with her father. She wrote him a letter at age twenty-one, as a birthday gift. No response. She heard crack cocaine gripped him. He lives perhaps three miles away, but Yasmine doesn't bump into him on the street, at the gas station, or in the corner grocery store. "I don't expect people to have sympathy for me. I don't complain. I make sure nothing happens to my kids."

But the demons are still there. During our interview, she vacillates between professing love and hate for her father. It's as if she is clasping a daisy and plucking the petals one by one, reciting "He loves me, he loves me not." Yasmine doesn't blame her father for her strip-club career.

We sit at the bar for a couple of hours. At one point she pauses. "It's hard to talk about," she says, sipping her second Purple Rain. The relationship is complex as calculus. "You don't know what it's like to be abused. It's a connection you can't understand. We were one person. He had a stroke one night. I spent the night out and I woke up that morning throwing up."

Moments later she says, "I can't see myself talking to him. I would kill him."

Recently her grandmother told Yasmine that her grandfather had sexually molested her father during childhood.

Like Pecola in Toni Morrison's *The Bluest Eye*, Yasmine has dreamed of being white because she hated what she saw in the mirror. Pecola and Yasmine might have been friends. Their abuse started at the same age. Both carried babies. Both dealt with drunk-ards as daddies. Both tried disappearing into their own misery. But only one knew her pregnancy wasn't the result of her father—and she found that out only after her labor.

Yasmine says she hated black men and never dated them until meeting her husband, a police officer. Her husband encourages her to seek therapy; she's resisting.

"My therapy is conquering the world. I want to get out of stripping. I'm tired," she says, explaining that her goal is to work with sexually abused children. But for several years stripping sustained her more than family and friends. Stripping gave her energy when she was emotionally sapped.

"Without this I wouldn't have nothing. When I dance I let my anger go. Just put it on stage. I let the anger flow."

I walked in a young lady and came out a woman.
　　　　　　　　—Diamond, in *The Players Club*

Sam's father stares at her from a frayed color photo. The photo captures a short, charming man wearing standard 1970s gear: butterfly collar, small Afro. She thinks he looks suave. Her father also lives in second- and thirdhand stories about a man from South Carolina, sweet as Godiva when sober, violent as a repeat offender when drunk.

Sam's parents didn't walk down the aisle, and her father deserted the family for good well before Sam's first birthday. She's been told he was a womanizer who beat her mother and destroyed Sam's baby clothes in one of his rageful fits. Put together, the information Sam knows about her father wouldn't fill a one-page letter. A last name didn't legally bind them. She doesn't know his birthday.

For years, she didn't think it mattered much. Growing up in a rough neighborhood in Maryland without a father was the norm. Her siblings and mother were a good support system. She said she never felt his absence. "I didn't want for school clothes. There were gifts under the Christmas tree. My mom sacrificed.... I never missed him."

Her mother frequently asked if she wanted to contact her father. Sam vaguely recalls going to a woman's house, probably his girlfriend's, and waiting outside for her father. He never came. As a teenager, Sam butted heads with her mother, who always worked more than one job and ran a tight ship. Sam rebelled against her mother's strictness by running away. After high school, she worked at Chuck E. Cheese's and enrolled in hairdressing school. Coerced by a friend to dance together on an amateur strip night, Sam got hooked. She could use the money. "I felt, hey, I have a nice body. The men can't touch me." Sam dropped out of hairdressing school. Dancing consumed her as she signed up for double shifts, hoarding up to one thousand dollars a night. She dressed in elaborate costumes dotted with sequins and ruffles.

"I became really, really good at it. I had a very small waist back then and a large rear end. I had to learn to use what I had. I could move it and shake it any kind of way." Her stage name was Pleazure, and she stripped to Sade and Prince, used slow music and feathers like Josephine Baker, earning titles such as "Miss Buns" and "Rumpshaker of D.C."

Sam's family hated it. Chris Rock would have been proud of her older brothers. They literally tried to haul her off the stage. Bouncers wouldn't let the brothers into clubs. The quick, easy money laced Sam in nice threads and furnished apartments. She recalls popping Ecstasy pills and drinking a lot to get through most nights.

Then she met her future husband. He was running around in the strip club he owned, smacking dancers on the rear. She'd told him she'd work a couple of nights at the club for extra money. Backstage, he laid his hand on her behind and Sam thought, I am the Rumpshaker of D.C., this is so beneath me. But she needed the money. Love grew, and she became his main girlfriend.

After a while, though, they both grew tired of the scene.

"I was so young, but I had already seen so much," she says. Dancers being stalked and killed. Girls getting locked up, raped, robbed, beaten. Alcoholism, drug abuse, degradation, the humiliation, the misery all had taken their toll. One Sunday, they went to a church service led by a minister who had been visiting them in one of her boyfriend's clubs. When the minister asked if anyone wanted to pledge their life to God, Sam felt her hand rising. She looked over, and her future husband's hand was already in the air.

Two weeks later, they were baptized. A week after that, they had their marriage license. Soon, Sam retired her dancing boots. Her husband gave up his strip clubs and dancers. The pair married, and for a while they operated a go-go gospel dance club. They had a baby—a son.

Still, Sam wishes her toddler-aged son could know his grandfather. Questions about her father nag at her every day. "I still don't know how to love men. I'm not really content. I'm never fully happy," Sam says, admitting that her discontent includes her marriage. Today she recognizes the void her father left.

Years ago, when she encountered one of her half sisters in the mall and learned that their dad had died, Sam just blinked and kept stepping. But lately the questions have grown more insistent. How did he grow up? What was he like? Why did he leave? Does he love her? In late winter 2005, Sam was about to embark on a Down South pilgrimage to meet her father's people and place flowers on his grave.

Sam doesn't look to the man in the photograph for her choices. "I can honestly say the family filled that void to the best of their ability. I can't put that blame there."

She runs alone, and damn it's cold.
No love in her life
Precious eyes to behold.

—unpublished poem by Jackie

Jackie (not her real name) has kept a journal since age eight, inspired by *The Diary of a Young Girl*, by Anne Frank. She is open about the poetry but is not ready to release the prose about her father. On the surface, her childhood looked as comfortable as fresh laundry. She was reared in an upper-middle-class Los Angeles family. Besides being given material goods, Jackie studied ballet, jazz, and tap dance. Her father was in politics, mother a school administrator.

But there were secrets.

When Jackie was four, her step-grandfather masturbated while she sat on his lap eating ice cream. A male friend of the family performed oral sex on her as part of his babysitting duties. Her father pressed her hand on his erection and inappropriately touched her body. Her mother, who was bipolar, ignored Jackie's pleas.

Jackie is now in her mid-twenties, and irrespective of the therapists who say a child can never be blamed for sexual abuse, she still blames herself. She describes the abuse as a power play, waffling about whether molestation is even the right word for what happened. "I remember turning it into a barter. You better buy me toys. Instead of [being] a shrinking violet and being the victim, I turned it into prostitution. Since you're going to do this, I realize I had power. I'm going to get toys out of it and I'm going to scream. I let myself get molested," she says. In her young mind she wielded power by accepting Barbie dolls, miniature fur coats, shiny bikes, and video games.

The abuse continued until she was about twelve. The so-called family friend and the step-grandfather had abused other cousins and were punished through the court system. The law never caught up with her father. She had to put a stop to it herself. "I started getting really mean and crazy. I'd threaten him: 'You have to fucking stop doing this.' I'd cry and scream and get hysterical. I'd take his hand and shove his hand off of me. I made it so difficult. The last straw for me was when he asked to look at my breast. He was not mean about it. He was very polite and nice."

She lost her virginity at age twelve and a half "to some stupid-ass boy in junior high because I wanted to be popular." Jackie's teenage years were tumultuous in a different way; hormones kicked in and her youthfulness clouded her judgment. By then her parents had divorced, and she and her mother constantly fought. She had virtually no criteria for sex—he just had to have a penis. In high school she went piercing berserk, putting holes in her nose, tongue, nipples, and stomach.

Jackie enrolled at a local university, and she took up Ecstasy, cocaine, and weed. After more combustion with her mother, Jackie moved out, dropped out of school, and took refuge in a hotel. Stripping appeared to be the natural next move.

"I already knew the stripping game. I don't know how to be a waitress, struggle with plates. I was very cute. I had fake boobs already."

Jackie parlayed her years of dance lessons into elaborate stage shows, dancing naked in tennis shoes to Nelly or in stilettos to 112, earning up to $1,500 a night. "I actually gained self-esteem after I was a stripper. Prior, I'd fuck anybody. I realized I had worth. Without my personality, my body itself had some value. I started to think if my body had value then my mind has value and then the spirit has value," Jackie says.

"My dad knew I stripped. He acted like he wasn't happy. I said, 'What the fuck are you going to do, give me money?' What could he say? I wasn't really connected to family. I was in an abusive relationship. Had I not been molested, I might not have stripped."

Before Jackie's epiphany about her self-worth, she spiraled in myriad directions. Asked about her prostitution, she rejects the label and takes a conciliatory posture, as she did with her childhood sexual abuse. "I hesitate to call it 'turning tricks.' It was bartering for goods and services, an extension of what I've been doing my whole life. I don't like the connotation of prostitution and I don't know if society is progressive enough to know the difference. I cared for gentlemen friends. Sometimes I wouldn't have sex," she says.

An overdose changed Jackie's mind about stripping. She woke up one morning not knowing how she got home and feeling as though her life was withering away. After more than a year of stripping, Jackie stopped cold turkey. Soon she reached out to her parents, who initiated family therapy. She continues her counseling because she craves a healthy romantic relationship.

Her dad apologized but plays dumb about the molestation. Jackie harbors no resentment. They are at peace. She returned to college and is poised to graduate. Her dad pays her tuition and apartment rent. They are normal as they can be.

"My dad is my hero. I respect him as a man. I'll always, always love and respect my father. Now that there are boundaries, I can forgive. I understand his frailties."

How much money was enough? Or would it never be enough?
It was time to cut her losses and move on.
                            —Shannon Holmes, *Bad Girlz*

Rena, twenty-five, a kindergarten teacher, thinks her daddy looks like Ron O'Neal from *Superfly*, with his long muttonchop sideburns. He transformed himself from a small-town Ohio boy into a big-city Detroit music producer who dabbled in real estate. He always smelled good: Obsession, Lagerfeld, and Fahrenheit, the colognes lingered on his collar. And he had charisma for days. "People looked up to him," Rena recalls. "He always had cronies or flunkies, people who did things for him, have his back."

Her father and her mother, a backup singer, never married, but they did cohabitate for a time, splitting up after Rena's tenth birthday. Her daddy showered her with love, advice, and presents. "I still had strong morals and ethics. I didn't want for a whole lot," says Rena.

Growing up in Michigan, she basked in her father's attention. When he introduced her to his friends and girlfriends, he'd brag, "This is my number one girl." He told her she was a race apart from everyone else. "You're a thoroughbred," he'd say. And he encouraged her to work like one, too. Be a hustler, he'd counsel. Have more than one job.

Rena took this advice to heart. By high school, she always held down at least two jobs: paper routes, washing dishes. Flipping through the television channels, Rena watched girls in strip club commercials rocking coiffed weaves, long lashes, and a Jayne Kennedy aura. "I thought I could look like that," Rena recalls. During her senior year of high school, she and a friend caked on lipstick, mascara, and eye shadow, arrived at a club, and lied to the doorman about their age. Inside, Rena said she stared like a pervert at one of the dancers, mesmerized by her body and stage presence. Noticing the teen's infatuation, the dancer became her stripper fairy godmother, giving a quick lesson on how to use the bottom of her feet to alter her body into a seductive force.

"I've always been that thick girl, big hips and big booty," Rena says. "I was always insecure but guys said it was hot." Rena vowed that when she turned eighteen, she'd do it for real. "I thought I could look like that. They were everything a man wanted." When it came time to pick a stage name, "Goldie" was the natural choice—the name of the lead character in the blaxploitation flick *The Mack*. Goldie demanded respect, just like her daddy. It's an unconscious occupational bond she has with her father.

Rena ventured away to a state school for college, and as she acclimated herself to studies and dorm life, she began plotting a side gig stripping. On a weekend trip home, she entered an amateur contest. She was nervous, but she recalled what her fairy godmother had taught her. *Your ass is your biggest asset.* It worked. Clients tossed money her way and she won the $250 contest. "Once you see that attention, it felt good." It opened up a lifestyle of Tiffany jewelry, holiday splurging, and shopping sprees.

Throughout the college years and beyond, Rena remained close to her father. When she felt like quitting school, he admonished her for crying too much about her difficulties. When she got pregnant by a professional athlete who insisted on an abortion, her father had a man-to-man talk with him. Rena herself decided not to have the baby. Once, when she was home from college, her dad discovered a shoebox full of singles stacked more than five-hundred-dollar high. "You aren't dancing on tables, are you?" he asked. She dodged the question, and he swiftly took her to the bank to open an account. But soon she was applying for a city-issued stripper dance card.

Rena used to marvel at Diamond, the heroine of the film *The Players Club*. But Rena has carved out her own place on the stripper stage as she transforms into her alter ego.

Toffee-colored Goldie disrobes at a club in the 'hood on Detroit's east side. Drug dealers and felons commune with each other, gawking at girls on stage. There's no visible champagne room, and the tiny space has the mores of a neighborhood bar. The DJ spins R. Kelly and the latest rap hits, weaving in Jill Scott and Goapele. Goldie looks bored on a random Friday night. While her G-string-wearing coworkers are carelessly whispering to customers between sets on stage, she parks at the bar, sipping water. When she does give a lap dance, Goldie appears aloof and faraway, her back toward the patron. Maybe she's thinking of her next lesson plan or out-of-state vacation. Her expression screams *Let me give this nigga a dance and keep it moving.*

She tries to keep reality and fantasy separate, at least somewhat.

Rena has never left the strip club with a customer for a midnight romp back at his place. But she hooks up with guys later. It's landed her free cruises and Las Vegas junkets. "If I know you like me, I will play you off. I'll play guys to get my hair done and bills paid. If I feel like sex, yes, but not as a barter.

"It's all a form of prostitution. Guys already have a perception. No one wants to hear how educated I am, that I'm a schoolteacher. You play them before they play you. They're already expecting a freak in bed. Treat them like a trick. No kisses. Oral is out. No affection."

Later, Goldie admits: "I wonder why I still do it. I make a good living [teaching]." She answers her own question. "It's the attention. It's a big part of why I like it. I was greedy. Enough was never enough." Sometimes she pulls in five hundred dollars a night for a few hours of work.

For five years Goldie has stripped at the same joint, where she is now probably the most senior dancer. Rena has never fully revealed the source of her moonlighting funds to her father.

When a friend of her father's saw her in the club and threatened to expose her, she issued a preemptive strike. She told her dad she'd been somewhere she shouldn't have. It's your business, he told her. End of discussion. "He raised me to take things to the grave. People don't have to know everything."

Goldie hasn't succumbed to drugs in her strip world. She does live a double life, waking up every morning to teach the alphabet to five-year-olds. She's in counseling now, and something happened to her several years ago that makes her question how long she'll be able to stay in the game. An intruder broke into the home Rena and her mother lived in and brutally raped them both. The rapist ripped her skin, and afterward Rena had trouble sitting.

BEST SEX WRITING 2006

Since then, she's tried to tuck away the incident. "It didn't affect me. Yes, physically. But I didn't want it to hold me back. It was just sex."

She didn't see the man's face, but she has a good idea where they may have been introduced. After the attack, he whispered "Goldie" in her ear.

The Nutty Confessor
Michelle Orange

The summer I turned eighteen I decided to stop screwing around, as it were, and lose my virginity. When my best friend Judy lost hers at sixteen, mine gained the inscrutable status of the parabolic equations annoying us every Tuesday morning out in the boonies at the only strict uniform school in London, Ontario. We also boasted the highest pregnancy rate. Though I think Judy failed geometry, she was a tireless number cruncher when it came to my prospects: I was given hard deadlines and I worked toward them prodigiously, like the recovering prodigy I was.

My categorical failure is still a mystery to me; boys were supposed to prefer sex to breathing, and if you subscribed to the received wisdom of the french fry line, I was getting more action than a collection plate on Good Friday. That's right, I'm Catholic, and I still couldn't give it away. Judy and I had a list, I am quite ashamed to say, and I spent a great deal of my free time systematically maneuvering each and every one of its entries into varying degrees of compromise. Some girls play volleyball after school; I just tried to score. Yet every time I pinned my itemized prey to the floor either I lost interest or they did. Secretly I assumed it was only going to happen when I was in love, but not so secretly I predicted what a pain in the ass that would be.

Eventually I reached the end of my list and had to switch high schools. At my new, non-Catholic arts school downtown I imagined cute boys, unburdened by underpants and other bogus tenets of the establishment, flowing through the halls like Chris Cornell's alpha mane. I was reaching the tail end of a very pronounced blond period, so when I saw Mark unlocking his bike by the smoke pit, his brilliant, hot-buttered hair falling in loose waves waaaaay down his back, I thought, *Ohhhhh*. And then, *Okay*.

All semester I kept my eye on Mark and he kept his eye on his bike. He was enigmatic, reportedly older, and maybe the best-looking human being I had ever seen. It was an ethereal kind of beauty, androgynous to the point of angelic, and it made my heart ache with that special brand of teen magazine longing you experience when you're eleven. With great patience and the cunning of a frustrated ninja, I made a plan. For months I made do with mere sightings, and I was rewarded with a turn in my favor: Mark got a job at the divey rock club my friends and I frequented. I also had three concurrent deadlines: I was graduating, turning eighteen, and moving across the country to British Columbia. Something had to give.

Poor Mark. He must have had dorkball girls like me following him around every minute of the day, fresh, unfocused need coming off us like paint fumes. He was very, very shy, with the kindest, warmest blue eyes; their lids sloped a bit at the sides, as though lightly stroked by sadness. I was completely elated when he asked me to stick around at the bar one night and tried to conceal my glee as he let his hand graze my shoulder whenever he passed. I chatted up the bouncers to try to distract them from the obvious pickup—gaining blatancy as the bar drained its slouchy dregs—with Mark sheepishly stacking barstools behind me. He was house-sitting for his parents, so we took a car to deepest suburbia, he showed me his old room, put me to bed with his eleven-year-old cat, kissed my forehead, and went downstairs to sleep on the couch.

It was all perfectly pleasant and perfectly perplexing. He called, but never to make a date, and I was too proud to complain. A couple of weeks later, after a night downtown with Judy, I suggested she drop me, like some sort of drunken CIA operative, in the East End—Mark's neighborhood. For the only time in my whole life this crude maneuver worked, and as I was walking back downtown to catch a bus my intended came riding toward me on that goddamn bike. I didn't have to fake my surprise, and he seemed pleased to see me. We walked to his friend's house for yet another drink, and at the kitchen table, chin in hand, I grew unexpectedly bold. I kicked my foot out of its shoe and curled my toes around his, lazily drumming my fingers against my cheek. He smiled and announced that we were leaving.

I learned early that you have to keep looking at people when you get the chance, and so, sitting on the floor of his tiny apartment in the bad part of town, I looked at Mark as he stood over me and pulled off his shirt. I wondered if my foot had written a check that the rest of me might not be able to cash, but even that idea turned me on.

He sat on the couch and I stayed on the floor, resting my head against his knee. He began to stroke my hair with a tenderness that was wholly unjustifiable, the kind of tenderness that can make a person cry. It made me calm and confused.

I turned to look up at him, and found his pretty, kitten face warmed up with that same, curious affection. I sat up and moved between his knees, leaning in and up to kiss him, and then I was kissing him, and it was heaven. I was feeling oddly powerful, not at all how I expected to feel, and then I was feeling Mark trembling. I kissed through it at first, finding it to be the most endearing thing imaginable, but it grew stronger, until I felt his shoulders shuddering in my hands. He pulled away from me, embarrassed, and said he was sorry, then stood and went into the bathroom to get some water.

He returned and we sat on the couch, where I just smiled and held in my breath. Moments later we were on his bed in the next room. It was barely wider than his shoulders, with a white bedspread covered in little nubs of fabric, like Braille. I wasn't feeling very powerful anymore—my own clothing piled on the floor was like kryptonite to me in those days—and as soon as I lost my shirt I wanted him to take over.

And he did, kind of. But in the bedroom we no longer seemed to fit. We lost it. I wanted to kiss him but his face seemed very far away; as I straddled his waist, his hands held me up and away, posed like a statue. I ran out of options—I can only stand to be looked at for so long—and unbuckled his pants, but before I really got anywhere he rose and put me on my stomach, face down on the tiny bed. He said he was going to give me "a massage," and that made me feel a little defeated. The preliminaries were starting to grate, and I trafficked exclusively in preliminaries. That's called a Catholic education.

Mark prodded away at my kidneys, and I felt him growing harder against me as his hands tugged down at my underpants. "Are you liking this?" he inquired, all fingertips and courtesy. All I wanted, from age fourteen to twenty, was to have a boyfriend, ideally a boyfriend of the all-that-stupid-old-shit type, but failing that (and it always failed that), to at least have sex. I didn't know why everyone else got to have one, or why everyone else got to have sex, and in that moment I grew conclusively tired of giving a shit.

And so I was more exhausted than relaxed when I heard myself mutter, for no particular reason, "I'm a virgin." I felt Mark freeze in mid-knead. "Are you serious?" he asked, darkly. "Mm-hm," I replied peacefully, face still mashed to the pillow. What a pervert I was. It was Mark's turn to feel defeated; he dismounted the small of my back and stretched out at my side. When I awoke and found his lovely, spindly body arranged in a perfect tableau of sleep on the couch, I smacked my forehead hard enough to rouse him.

I didn't see Mark again until New Year's Eve. I was back in town after a disastrous stint on the West Coast wherein I was robbed blind, got mixed up with the Hawaiian mafia, and had an earring torn clean through my earlobe behind the Kitsilano youth hostel. "There goes your modeling career," my roommate had said, prying my hand from my ear as I lay curled up on the bottom bunk.

At the bar with my friends, I drank too much and became maudlin. Mark finished his shift and offered to walk me home, across the moon-blue blister of snow rising over the park. I would return to Vancouver in two days. "Don't make me go back there," I murmured.

We stopped walking but the snow kept falling, and that made me a little dizzy. I wasn't feeling powerful anymore, or innocent, or anything. Mark took my face in his hands and said, "What am I going to do with you?" I knew the answer to that, but trained my eyes on his lips anyway, hoping they would move again, and tell me I was wrong.

The Cuddle Puddle of Stuyvesant High School
Alex Morris

Alair is wearing a tight white tank top cut off above the hem to show her midriff. Her black cargo pants graze the top of her combat boots, and her black leather belt is studded with metal chains that drape down at intervals across her hips. She has long blonde curls that at various times have been dyed green, blue, red, purple, and orange. ("A mistake," she says. "Even if you mean to dye your hair orange, it's still a mistake.") Despite the fact that she's fully clothed, she seems somehow exposed, her baby fat lingering in all the right places. Walking down the sterile, white halls of Stuyvesant High School, she creates a wave of attention. She's not the most popular girl in school, but she is well known. "People like me," she wrote in an instant message. "Well, most of them."

Alair is headed for the section of the second-floor hallway where her friends gather every day during their free tenth period for the "cuddle puddle," as she calls it. There are girls petting girls and girls petting guys and guys petting guys. She dives into the undulating heap of backpacks and blue jeans and emerges between her two best friends, Jane and Elle, whose names have been changed at their request. They are all sixteen, juniors at Stuyvesant. Alair slips into Jane's lap, and Elle reclines next to them, watching, cat-eyed. All three have hooked up with each other. All three have hooked up with boys—sometimes the same boys. But it's not that they're gay or bisexual, not exactly. Not always.

Their friend Nathan, a senior with John Lennon hair and glasses, is there with his guitar, strumming softly under the conversation. "So many of the girls here are lesbian or have experimented or are confused," he says.

Ilia, another senior boy, frowns at Nathan's use of labels. "It's not lesbian or bisexual. It's just, whatever..."

Since the school day is winding down, things in the hallway are starting to get rowdy. Jane disappears for a while and comes back carrying a pint-size girl over her shoulder. "Now I take her off and we have gay sex!" she says gleefully, as she parades back and forth in front of the cuddle puddle. "And it's awesome!" The hijacked girl hangs limply, a smile creeping to her lips. Ilia has stuffed papers up the front of his shirt and prances around on tiptoe, batting his eyes and sticking out his chest. Elle is watching, enthralled, as two boys lock lips across the hall. "Oh, my," she murmurs. "Homoerotica. There's nothing more exciting than watching two men make out." And everyone is talking to another girl in the puddle who just "came out," meaning she announced that she's now open to sexual overtures from both boys and girls, which makes her a minor celebrity, for a little while.

When asked how many of her female friends have had same-sex experiences, Alair answers, "All of them." Then she stops to think about it. "All right, maybe eighty percent. At least eighty percent of them have experimented. And they still are. It's either to please a man, or to try it out, or just to be fun, or 'cause you're bored, or just 'cause you like it…whatever."

With teenagers there is always a fair amount of posturing when it comes to sex, a tendency to exaggerate or trivialize, innocence mixed with swagger. It's also true that the "puddle" is just one clique at Stuyvesant, and that Stuyvesant can hardly be considered a typical high school. It attracts the brightest public-school students in New York, and that may be an environment conducive to fewer sexual inhibitions. "In our school," Elle says, "people are getting a better education, so they're more open-minded."

That said, the Stuyvesant cuddle puddle is emblematic of the changing landscape of high school sexuality across the country. This past September, when the National Center for Health Statistics released its first survey in which teens were questioned about their sexual behavior, 11 percent of American girls polled in the fifteen-to-nineteen demographic claimed to have had same-sex encounters—the *same* percentage of all women ages fifteen to forty-four who reported same-sex experiences, even though the teenagers have much shorter sexual histories. It doesn't take a Stuyvesant education to see what this means: More girls are experimenting with each other, and they're starting younger. And this is a conservative estimate, according to Ritch Savin-Williams, a professor of human development at Cornell who has been conducting research on same-sex-attracted adolescents for over twenty years. Depending on how you phrase the questions and how you define sex between women, he believes that "it's possible to get up to 20 percent of teenage girls."

Of course, what can't be expressed in statistical terms is how teenagers think about their same-sex interactions. Go to the schools, talk to the kids, and you'll see that somewhere along the

line this generation has started to conceive of sexuality differently.
Ten years ago in the halls of Stuyvesant you might have found a few
goth girls kissing goth girls, kids on the fringes defiantly bucking the
system. Now you find a group of vaguely progressive but generally
mainstream kids for whom same-sex intimacy is standard operating
procedure. "It's not like, *Oh, I'm going to hit on her now.* It's just kind
of like, you come up to a friend, you grab their ass," Alair explains.
"It's just, like, our way of saying hello." These teenagers don't feel
as though their sexuality has to define them, or that they have to
define it, which has led some psychologists and child development
specialists to label them the "post-gay" generation. But kids like
Alair and her friends are in the process of working up their own
language to describe their behavior. Along with gay, straight, and
bisexual, they'll drop in new words, some of which they've coined
themselves: *polysexual, ambisexual, pansexual, pansensual, polyfide,
bi-curious, bi-queer, fluid, metroflexible, heteroflexible, heterosexual with
lesbian tendencies*—or, as Alair puts it, "just sexual." The terms are
designed less to achieve specificity than to leave all options open.

   To some it may sound like a sexual Utopia, where labels have
been banned and traditional gender roles surpassed, but it's a complicated place to be. Anyone who has ever been a girl in high
school knows the vicissitudes of female friendships. Add to that a
sexual component and, well, things get interesting. Take Alair and
her friend Jane, for example. "We've been dancing around each
other for, like, three years now," says Alair. "I'd hop into bed with
her in a second." Jane is tall and curvy, with green eyes and faint
dimples. She thinks Alair is "amazing," but she's already had a female friendship ruined when it turned into a romantic relationship,
so she's reluctant to let it happen again. Still, they pet each other
in the hall, flirt, kiss, but that's it, so far. "Alair," Jane explains, "is
literally in love with everyone and in love with no one."

"Relationships are a bitch, dude."

Alair is having lunch with Jane, Elle, and their friend Nathan at a little Indian place near Jane's Upper West Side apartment. Jane has been telling the story of her first lesbian relationship: She fell for a girl who got arrested while protesting the Republican National Convention (very cool), but the girl stopped calling after they spent the night together (very uncool).

"We should all be single for the rest of our lives," Alair continues. "And we should all have sugar daddies." As the only child of divorced parents, Alair learned early that love doesn't always end in happily ever after and that sex doesn't always end in love.

Nathan looks across the table at her and nods knowingly. He recently broke up with a girl he still can't get off his mind, even though he wasn't entirely faithful when they were together. "I agree. I wholeheartedly agree," he says.

"I *disagree*," says Elle, alarmed. She's the romantic of the group, a bit naive, if you ask the others.

"Well," Nathan says. "You're, like, the only one in a happy relationship right now, so…"

Alair cracks up. "Happy? Her man is gayer than I am!" (Jane, the sarcastic one, has a joke about this boy: "He's got one finger left in the closet, and it's in Elle, depending on what time it is.")

"But at least she's happy," argues Nathan.

"When I'm single, I say I'm happy I'm single, and when I'm in a relationship I seem happy in the relationship. Really, I'm filled with angst!" says Elle.

Nathan rolls his eyes. "Anyone who says they're filled with angst is definitely *not* filled with angst."

He's got a point. In her brand-new sneakers and her sparkly barrettes, Elle is hardly a poster child for teenage anxiety. She makes A's at Stuyvesant, babysits her cousins, and is engaging in a way that will go over well in college interviews. Then again, none of them are bad kids. Sure, they drink and smoke and party, but in a couple of years, they'll be drinking and smoking and partying at Princeton or MIT. They had to be pretty serious students even to get into Stuyvesant, which accepts only about 3 percent of its applicants. And when they're not studying, they're going to music lessons, SAT prep, debate practice, Japanese class, theater rehearsal, or some other résumé-building extracurricular activity.

Their sexual behavior is by no means the norm at their school; Stuyvesant has some three thousand students, and Alair's group numbers a couple dozen. But they're also not the only kids at school who experiment with members of the same sex. "Other people do it, too," said a junior who's part of a more popular crowd. "They get drunk and want to be a sex object. But that's different. Those people aren't bisexual." Alair and her friends, on the other hand, are known as the "bi clique." In the social strata, they're closer to the cool kids than to the nerds. The boys have shaggy hair and T-shirts emblazoned with the names of sixties rockers. The girls are pretty and clever and extroverted. Some kids think they're too promiscuous. One student-union leader told me, "It's weird. It's just sort of incestuous." But others admire them. Alair in particular is seen as a kind of punk-rock queen bee. "She's good-looking, and she does what she wants," said a senior boy. "That's an attractive quality."

"The interesting kids kind of gravitate towards each other," Elle had explained earlier. "A lot of them are heteroflexible or bisexual or gay. And what happens is, like, we're all just really comfortable around each other."

Still, among her friends, Elle's ideas are the most traditional. Her first kiss with a girl was at Hebrew school. Since then, she's made out with girls frequently but dated only guys.

"I've always been the marrying type," she says to the table. "Not just 'cause it's been forced on me, but 'cause it's a good idea. I really want to have kids when I grow up."

"Have mine," offers Alair.

"I will," Elle coos in her best sultry voice. "Anything for you, Alair."

Jane blinks quickly, something she has a habit of doing when she's gathering her thoughts. "They will probably have the technology by the time we grow up that you two could have a baby together."

"But, like, if Alair doesn't want to birth her own child, I could."

"I'll birth it," Alair says, sighing. "I just want you to raise it and pay for it and take care of it and never tell it that I'm its parent. 'Cause, I mean, that would scar a child for life. Like, the child would start convulsing." Everyone laughs.

"You'd be an awesome mom, I think," says Elle. Her own mom puts a lot of pressure on her to date a nice Jewish boy. Once, Elle asked her, " 'Mom, what if I have these feelings for girls?' and she said, 'Do you have feelings for boys too?' I'm like, 'Yeah.' And she's like, 'Then you have to ignore the ones you have for girls. If you can be straight, you have to be straight.' " Elle asked to go by a nickname because she hasn't told her mother that she's not ignoring those feelings.

Even as cultural acceptance of gay and bisexual teenagers grows, these kids are coming up against an uncomfortable generational divide. In many of their families, the 'It's fine, as long as it's not my kid' attitude prevails. Some of the parents take comfort in the belief that this is just a phase their daughters will grow out of. Others take more drastic measures. Earlier this year at Horace Mann, when one girl's parents found out that she was having a relationship with another girl, they searched her room, confiscated her love letters, and even had the phone company send them transcripts of all her text messages. Then they informed her girlfriend's parents. In the end, the girls were forbidden to see each other outside school.

Even Jane, whose parents know about her bisexuality and are particularly well suited to understanding it (her mother teaches a college course in human sexuality), has run up against the limits of their liberal attitudes. They requested that she go by her middle name in this story. "My mom thinks I'm going to grow up and be ashamed of my sexuality," she says. "But I *won't*."

To these kids, homophobia is as socially shunned as racism was to the generation before them. They say it's practically the one thing that's not tolerated at their school. One boy who made disparaging remarks about gay people has been ridiculed and taunted, his belongings hidden around the school. "We're a creative bunch when we hate someone," says Nathan. Once the tormenters, now the tormented.

Alair is one of the lucky ones whose parents don't mind her bisexual tendencies. Her dad is the president of a company that manages performance artists and her mom is a professional organizer. "My parents are awesome," she says. "I think they've tried to raise me slightly quirky, like in a very hippie little way, and it totally backfired on them."

"'Cause you ended up like a hippie?" Nathan asks.

"No, 'cause I went further than I think they wanted me to go." Despite the bravado, there's a sweetness to Alair. She sings in the Trinity Children's Choir. She does the dishes without being asked. She's a daddy's girl and her mother's confidante, though she hasn't always managed to skirt trouble away from home. She got kicked out of her middle school, Columbia Prep, after getting into an altercation with a girl who had been making her life miserable. ("I threw a bagel at her head, all right? I attacked her with a bagel.")

"My mom's like, 'Alair, I don't understand you. I want to be a parent to you but I have no control at all…. As a person you're awesome. You're hilarious, you entertain me, you're so cool. I would totally be your friend. But as your mother, I'm worried.' "

"I can't say I was pleased," her mother tells me about first learning of Alair's bisexual experimentation. "But I can't say I was upset either. I like that she's forthright about what she wants, that she values her freedom, that she takes care of herself. But I have all the trepidations a parent has when they learn their child is becoming sexually active."

Of course, none of these kids will have to deal with their parents quite this directly in another year or so—a fact of which they are all acutely aware. College is already becoming a pressing issue. Everyone thinks Elle is going to get into Harvard. "If I fail physics, my average drops like a stone," she frets. Alair and Nathan want to go to the same college, wherever that may be.

"You do realize," Alair tells him, "that, like, we're two of the most awesome people in the school."

"We would room," Nathan says. "We would totally room."

"Fuck yeah. But I'm gonna need a lock on my door for like, 'I'm bringing these five girls home, Nathan. What are you doing tonight?' " She mimics his voice. " 'I'm reading my book.' "

"Ouch!" Nathan scowls at her.

"It's the *Kama Sutra*!"

"Oh, right, right."

"I've actually read the *Kama Sutra*," Alair informs the table. "Some of that shit just isn't gonna work."

"I know!" says Jane. "We have three editions at my house."

"Like, I've tried it. You need a man that's like 'Argh!' " Alair pumps her arms up above her head. "I've got one of those guys, actually." She's talking about Jason, the boy she was hanging out with last night, another frequenter of the cuddle puddle. "He's so built."

"He's in love with you," Jane says drily.

"No, he's not!"

"Yes he is!"

"How could he *not* be in love with Alair?" Nathan reasons.

Jane nods in Alair's direction. "He bought you gum."

"He bought you gum." This cinches it for Nathan. "Yeah, he loves you. He wants you so in his underwear."

Alair looks at him blankly. "But he already has that. We're friends." There's no need to bring love into it.

But later, back at Jane's apartment, as the afternoon is turning to night, Alair has the look of, if not love, at least infatuation, as she waits in the hallway for the elevator to take her back down. Only it's not Jason she's saying good-night to—it's Jane. "You make my knees weak," she says. And then, to cut the tension: "I showered for you and everything." She leans in and gives Jane a kiss.

It practically takes a diagram to plot all the various hookups and connections within the cuddle puddle. Elle's kissed Jane and Jane's kissed Alair and Alair's kissed Elle. And then from time to time Elle hooks up with Nathan, but really only at parties, and only when Bethany isn't around, because Nathan really likes Bethany, who doesn't have a thing for girls but doesn't have a problem with girls who do, either. Alair's hooking up with Jason (who "kind of" went out with Jane once), even though she sort of also has a thing for Hector, who Jane likes, too—though Jane thinks it's totally boring when people date people of the same gender. Ilia has a serious girlfriend, but girls were hooking up at his last party, which was awesome. Molly has kissed Alair, and Jane's ex-girlfriend first decided she was bi while staying at Molly's beach house on Fire Island. Sarah sometimes kisses Elle, although she has a boyfriend—he doesn't care if she hooks up with other girls, since she's straight anyway. And so on.

Some of the boys hook up with each other, too, although in far fewer numbers than the girls. One of Alair's male friends explained that this is because, for guys, anything beyond same-sex kissing requires "more of a physical commitment." If a guy does hook up with other guys it certainly doesn't make the girls less likely to hook up with him; and the converse is obviously true.

Of course, the definition of "hooking up" is as nebulous as the definition of "heteroflexible." A catchall phrase for anything from "like, exchanging of saliva" to intercourse, it's often a euphemism for oral sex. But rules are hazy when you're talking about physical encounters between two girls. As Alair puts it, "How do you define female sex? It's difficult. I don't know what the bases are. Everyone keeps trying to explain the bases to me, but there's so many things that just don't fit into the base system. I usually leave it up to the other girl."

Elle elaborates by using herself as an example. At a recent party, she says, she "kissed five people and, like, hooked up with two going beyond kissing. One of them was a boy and one of them was a girl. The reason I started hooking up with the guy is because he was making out with this other guy and he came back and was like, 'I have to prove that I'm straight.' And I was standing right there. That's how it all began." The guy in question became her boyfriend that night; even though the relationship is all of a week old, she calls it her second "serious" relationship. "At least I'm intending for it to be serious." (It lasted eleven days.)

The cuddle puddle may be where a flirtation begins, but parties, not surprisingly, are where most of the real action takes place. In parentless apartments, the kids are free to "make the rounds," as they call it, and move their more-than-kissing hookups with both genders behind locked bathroom doors or onto coat-laden beds. Even for bisexual girls there is, admittedly, a *Girls Gone Wild* aspect to these evenings. Some girls do hook up with other girls solely to please the guys who watch, and it can be difficult to distinguish between the behavior of someone who is legitimately sexually interested and someone who wants to impress the boy across the room. Alair is quick to disparage this behavior—"It kinda grosses me out. It can't be like, this could be fun…is anyone watching my chest heave?"—but Jane sees it as empowering. "I take advantage of it because manipulating boys is fun as hell. Boys make out with boys for our benefit as well. So it's not just one way. It's very fair."

She's not just making excuses. These girls have obliterated the "damned if you do, damned if you don't" stranglehold that has traditionally plagued high-school females. They set the sexual agenda for their group. And they expect reciprocation. "I've made it my own personal policy that if I'm going to give oral sex, I'm going to receive oral sex," says Jane. "Jane wears the pants in any relationship," Ilia says with a grin. "She wears the pants in *my* relationship, even though she's not part of it."

When the girls talk about other girls they sound like football players in a locker room ("The Boobie Goddesses of our grade are Natalie and Annette" or "Have you seen the Asian girl who wears that tiny red dress and those high red sneakers?" or "Carol is so hot! Why is she straight? I don't get it"), but there's little gossip about same-sex hookups—partly because the novelty has by now worn off, and partly because, as Alair puts it, "it's not assumed that a relationship will stem from it." It seems that even with all the same-sex activity going on, it's still hard for the girls to find other girls to actually date. Jane says this is because the girls who like girls generally like boys more, at least for dating. "A lot of girls are scared about trying to make a lesbian relationship work," she says. "There's this fear that there has to be the presence of a man or it won't work."

But dating gay girls isn't really an option either, because the cuddle-puddle kids are not considered part of the gay community. "One of the great things about bisexuality is that mainstream gay culture doesn't affect us as much," says Jane, "so it's not like bi boys feel that they have to talk with a lisp and walk around all fairylike, and it's not like girls feel like they have to dress like boys." The downside, she says, is that "gays feel that bis will cheat on them in a straight manner." In fact, there's a general impression of promiscuity that bisexual girls can't seem to shake. "The image of people who are bi is that they are sluts," says Jane. "One of the reasons straight boys have this bi-girls fantasy is that they are under the impression that bisexual girls will sleep with anything that moves and that's why they like both genders, because they are so sex-obsessed. Which isn't true."

If you ask the girls why they think there's more teenage bisexual experimentation happening today, Alair is quick with an explanation. "I blame television," she says. "I blame the media." She's partly joking, giving the stock answer. But there's obviously some truth to it. She's too young to remember a time when she couldn't turn on Showtime or even MTV and regularly see girls kissing girls. It's not simply that they're imitating what they've seen, it's that the stigma has been erased, maybe even transformed into cachet. "It's in the realm of possibilities now," as Ritch Savin-Williams puts it. "When you don't think of it as being a possibility, you don't do it. But now that it's out there, it's like, 'Oh, yeah, that could be fun.' " Of course, sexy TV shows would have no impact at all if they weren't tapping into something more innate. Perhaps, as research suggests, sexuality is more fluid for women than it is for men. Perhaps natural female intimacy opens the door to sexual experimentation at an age when male partners can be particularly unsatisfying. As one mother of a cuddle-puddle kid puts it, "Emotionally it's safer—it's difficult in this age group to hold onto your body. You're changing. There's a safety factor in a girl being with a girl." Then, laughing, she asked that her name be withheld. "*My* mother might read this."

It's true that girls have always experimented, but it's typically been furtive, kept quiet. The difference now is how these girls are flaunting it. It's become a form of exhibitionism, a way to get noticed at an age when getting noticed is what it's all about. And as rebellions go, it's pretty safe. Hooking up with girls won't get them pregnant. It won't hurt their GPA. It won't keep them out of honor societies, social groups, the Ivy League.

In the end, the Stuyvesant cuddle puddle might just be a trickle-down version of the collegiate "gay until graduation." On the other hand, these girls are experimenting at an earlier age, when their identities and their ideas about what they want in a partner are still being formed. Will it affect the way they choose to live their adult lives? Elle is determined to marry a man, but Alair and Jane are not so sure. Maybe they won't get married at all, they say, keep their options open. "I have no idea," says Alair. "I'm just sixteen."

A few weeks later, the guys are hanging out in Nathan's room. Jason is stretched out on the bed and Ilia is leaning back in a chair by the desk, and it's pretty clear that nothing much is happening this afternoon. Just some guitar playing, some lying about. Then the girls show up and things get more interesting. Alair and Jane have brought a couple of friends, Molly and Nikki. Molly doesn't know for sure if she's bisexual, but "I have my suspicions," she says; she's hooked up with Alair before. Nikki is with her friend Jared, whom she's sort of but not really dating. He makes out with boys but considers Nikki his "soul mate"; she's totally straight but kisses girls. "I kiss anything pretty, anything beautiful, anything worthwhile," she says.

Nikki runs her hands through Jane's hair. "You look awesome! I love this shirt. I love your hair." Jane crosses the room to sit in Alair's lap, and Alair wraps her arms around her. That reminds Nikki of something.

"Wait! Let me show you guys the next painting I'm doing," she says, pulling from her backpack a photograph of Alair asleep on the beach in a striped bikini. It's a sexy picture, and Nikki knows it.

Chinese food is ordered, guitars strummed, an ice cube is passed around and for no apparent reason everyone is required to put it down their pants. It's just another afternoon of casual flirtation. The boys showing off for the girls, the girls showing off for everyone. No strings attached. In theory, anyway. Most of the kids say they hate relationships, that they don't want to be tied down, that they want to be open to different possibilities and different genders from minute to minute, but there is a natural tendency—as natural perhaps as the tendency to experiment—to try to find connection. Like it or not, emotions get involved. If you look closer, you can see the hint of longing, the momentary pouting, the tiny jealousies. Jared can't take his eyes off Nikki, but Nikki seems interested mainly in Alair. Jason, too, is angling for Alair's attention, but Alair is once again focused on Jane. And Jane, well, Jane might actually be in love.

She is in a particularly good mood today, quick to smile, and even more quick to drop into conversation the name of the boy she recently started dating, a tall, good-looking senior and one of the most popular kids at Stuyvesant. Later, while rummaging for silverware, she casually mentions that they may start dating exclusively.

"Ugh!" Alair exclaims, grabbing her by the hips and pulling her away from the drawer. "What about me?"

"Let's put it this way," Jane counters, grinning and snatching up a fork. "I'm not interested in any other *guys*."

Still, it's clear that Jane really likes this guy. And Alair seems a little rattled. Her fortune cookie reads, "You are the master of every situation." Except perhaps this one.

Later, after the lamps have been switched on and the takeout eaten, both girls are on a love seat in the living room, leaning into each other, boys and dirty dishes strewn about. Jane starts showing off what she can do with her tongue, touching her nose with it, twisting it around, doing rolls. Everyone is impressed.

"My tongue gets a lot of practice," she says.

"Why don't you practice on me?" Alair demands. "I'll hook up with you." It's clear that she means more than kissing.

Jane blinks a few times. "I'm scared I'm going to be bad at it," she finally says. She's being coy, just putting her off, but there's a bit of sincerity to her nervousness.

"You won't be bad at it," Alair reassures her. She pulls Jane between her legs and starts giving her a massage, running her hands up and down her back, pushing her hair aside to rub her neck. When the massage is over, Jason comes over to Alair, grabs her hand, kisses it. For the rest of the evening, he stays close to her side, but she stays close to Jane.

The next day, when I meet up with Alair on her way to choir practice, she tells me that nothing ever happened with Jane that night. She's decided to give up on her. Jane's with someone else, it's official, and there's no room in the relationship for her. "But you know what," she says, mustering a smile. "They're, like, monogamous together, and I'm really happy for them. And being their friend and seeing them so happy together totally beats a fling." She pauses. "It really does."

An Ode to Ass:
Reflections on Sex Ed, Porn, and Perversity
Tristan Taormino

Fuck Abstinence

When I was in sixth grade, I went on my first date, with a guy named Mike. We walked to a pizza parlor. Over pepperoni slices and Cokes, we talked, although I have no memory of what we talked *about*. I know that I spent a lot of time worrying about what to wear; eventually I settled on my Sergio Valente jeans and a blue jacket. Afterward, he walked me back to my house. I remember that I liked him and had fun with him. On Monday at school, girls asked me for details, and the most pressing question seemed to be "Did you kiss?" I panicked: I forgot to kiss him. Later that week, the teacher separated the girls and boys and marched us into different classrooms. We watched a filmstrip about menstruation and reproduction. The teacher told us about fallopian tubes, ovaries, and tampons. I paid attention, but it had little relevance to my life since I was still stressing about not locking lips with Mike. Among my friends, I was one of the only ones who had even gone on a date. I was supposed to kiss him or let him kiss me, and in my genuine giddiness, I totally flubbed it. I've changed a lot in the twenty years since then, but so has an entire generation of young adults.

A study published in the journal *Pediatrics* in April 2005 found that 20 percent of ninth-graders surveyed had engaged in oral sex and 14 percent had had vaginal intercourse. The study confirmed what Oprah, Dr. Phil, and other major media personalities have called "an oral-sex epidemic" among kids as young as twelve. It's certainly alarming for parents that children are beginning to sexually experiment at a younger age than their generation or mine. Researchers concluded: "That so many adolescents are having oral sex and view it as safe, perceiving little or no risk resulting from engaging in oral sex, stresses the importance of needing more research on oral sex transmissibility rates and increased health education about oral sex."

What's more troubling is that this study was released in a year when the federal government allocated more money than ever—about $130 million—to "abstinence-only-until-marriage" sex education in schools. There are no comparable funds for other kinds of sex ed curricula. A study by Yale and Columbia researchers found that teens who take an abstinence pledge are more likely to engage in sexual activities other than vaginal intercourse; members of this same group were also less likely to use a condom in their first sexual experience and less likely to get tested for STDs. In an earlier study, the same research team found that 88 percent of teens who took the pledge had vaginal intercourse before marriage.

Last year, in a report on abstinence-only education, California representative Henry Waxman found that more than two-thirds of government-funded abstinence-only programs contain misleading or inaccurate information about sex. (Example: "A pregnancy occurs one out of every seven times that couples use condoms." In fact, condoms are up to 98 percent effective at preventing pregnancy when used correctly.) Clearly, abstinence-only education is problematic and ineffective.

But these studies also highlight that abstinence-only and other sex ed programs have a critical flaw in common: The focus is on "sex" defined either explicitly or implicitly as vaginal intercourse. The abstinence kids pledge not to have sex (vaginal intercourse) but do have oral sex, manual sex, and anal sex. The teens in the *Pediatrics* report who've had oral sex think it's not sex. That study also found that "adolescents did believe that they were more likely to experience pleasure from vaginal sex than from oral sex," a message promoted not only by sex ed, but by kids' peers and the media. Other forms of pleasure, especially female sexual pleasure, including clitoral stimulation, are not part of the discussion. Vaginal intercourse is the big deal, the one with physical and emotional repercussions—everything else is safe and breezy.

Don't get me wrong; abstinence should always be presented as an option. But the reality is that most kids are experimenting with some form of sex, and they need to know how their bodies work, how STDs are transmitted, and how to protect themselves. Most kids are still confused about basic anatomy and how someone gets pregnant. (More than 16 percent said there was a chance of getting pregnant through oral sex.) These teenagers become college students who attend my lectures and ask, "I can't come from vaginal intercourse—what's wrong with me?"

I propose a sex ed curriculum that honestly educates teenagers about the risks, responsibilities, and rewards of sex. Educators need to talk to actual teenagers and get their input about what will and won't be effective for them and their peers. Create a safe environment with an outside instructor, without teachers or other monitors in the room. Don't bring out the diagrams without also using three-dimensional, realistic models. Talk to teens in their own language rather than using clinical terms they cannot relate to. Let them ask anonymous questions so they don't feel pressure to act cool or knowledgeable around their peers. Show them how to use condoms, gloves, dental dams, and lube correctly, and have those items available. Give a reading packet that is accessible, informative, and sex positive, which they can take home for future reference. Use resources like Planned Parenthood's Teenwire.com and the independently run (read: underfunded) Scarleteen.com, two of the best sex ed websites for teens. Encourage parents to get involved. Don't just have them sign the permission slip; give them tools (like a class of their own) for talking to kids about sex, and encourage them to follow up.

We continue to do a great disservice to the teenagers in this country when it comes to sex education. The United States has the highest teen pregnancy rate and teen STD rate in the Western world. Teenagers are having sex. Teenagers are licking pussy, sucking cock, munching ass, finger-fucking, dry humping, and buttfucking. George Bush wants them to practice abstinence. Well, abstinence-only education sucks. When we deny that young people are sexual beings, withhold information and resources from them, and narrowly define sex to exclude all possibilities but one, we contribute to a new generation of sexually illiterate adults.

Private Dick

Two students at the University of Pennsylvania were having sex against a dorm room window without a shade. Apparently, several people took photos of the couple, and the images were circulated via e-mail and on various websites. A student who snapped a shot and posted it on his personal site was charged with several violations by the Office of Student Conduct. One charge was sexual harassment, based on a complaint from the female student (who believed she could be identified) that posting the image created a hostile environment for her. Debates raged in the student newspaper and online forums: Why was the photographer being charged with sexual harassment but the couple was not being charged with public lewdness? What about the shutterbug's right to free speech? If the two were putting on a show, how could they expect privacy? From the photos I've seen, it doesn't look like a case of a Peeping Tom with a telephoto lens. Pictures were taken in broad daylight, and although the couple was in a high-rise building, one look up let you see a whole lot. One person posted this comment on the *Daily Pennsylvanian* website: "You don't smash your buttocks up against a window unless you're looking for attention." I'll agree: The twosome wanted to be watched or wanted the possibility of being watched to exist. However, being an exhibitionist and having your exhibitionism photographed and published are two very different things.

I can't remember the first time I had public sex. I am not counting the times I had sex in a semipublic or public place where I could have been watched but wasn't—like in a car, at the beach, or in a park. I am talking about having sex in public to be seen. Was it when I went to a sex club in Florida during a leather conference? It might have been the night that I hooked up with a well-known sexpert couple at a sex party in Boston. As I recall, she fucked me on a couch, then I fisted her partner. It was the first time I used the female condom for anal penetration—and I remember thinking it was ironic that I was trying it out in a guy. Maybe it was at the porn-star orgy I was invited to, where I was one of only three nonporn people. (They called us "civilians.") I got to fuck a performer briefly until his girlfriend—who was doing someone else—kind of flipped out. I did hook up with a retired porn star who put almost her entire fist in my ass. Wow, the mid-'90s are already a blur.

I used to be an exhibitionist. I go-go-danced at dyke bars, where women stuck folded bills in my G-string. I had my pussy shaved onstage by a stranger as part of a performance. At a story-telling event, someone (another stranger) put a butt plug in my ass as I read my erotic story. I got pierced, poked, and paddled at kinky parties. I fucked my entire cast in the final scene of the first porn video I directed. I preferred to indulge my love of the spotlight while naked. I loved to fuck and be fucked while people looked on.

Maybe it's just a phase, but lately I'm not so gung ho to have sex in public. I still put things in people's orifices in front of a roomful of others—which I know looks a lot like sex—but I don't count that because it really is an educational thing. I mean wrists-and-ankles-strapped-to-a-bondage-table-while-hot-wax-is-dripped-on-my-tits public sex. Or face down, ass in the air, on a bed in a room with no door. Or lubed glove dripping as I lean over some hot number, her legs spread wide as she seemingly floats midair in a sling.

Thankfully, I still have plenty of opportunities to have public sex. But seeing a ten-thousand-square-foot dungeon and two hundred pairs of eyes doesn't do it for me like it used to. Public sex was exciting and validating, and it fed something in me that's no longer hungry. In the past, one of the thrills of public sex, especially at parties, was that I felt free to do whatever the fuck I wanted to. Whether in a corner or center stage, I was just another girl with tattoos and high heels getting off; I felt free. One of the last times I had anonymous sex in public, I found the entire encounter written up in my play-mate's blog, which wouldn't have been so disturbing if she hadn't used my full name without my permission. That felt icky.

These days, when I pick up a cane or slip off my panties in a public place, I feel an enormous weight on my shoulders. Like there are these expectations of me, as a sexpert, to give people a great show and to rock the world of whomever I am playing with. That kind of pressure, whether real or imagined, just kills my libido. Part of fucking in public is a performance, and for whatever reasons, I'm not in the mood to perform. That part of it distracts me and gets me out of the zone I need to be in. Right now, I want to go places in my sexual life that I am not ready to share with an audience. Some of those places are dark; others are goofy, tender, and complicated. I'm hesitant to do the things I want to in public because I feel too vulnerable.

Last week, the University of Pennsylvania Office of Student Conduct dropped all charges against the photographer who caught a moment of young lust and exhibitionism. According to several reports, the couple, especially the woman, is embarrassed and humiliated—which is really the opposite of how it could have gone down if the looking was fleeting rather than captured digitally. Some of the best public sex I've witnessed is when the opposite emotions are evident, and the woman feels incredibly empowered. When I watch a woman shed her inhibitions and bare herself for all to see, sometimes I envy her—she can embrace and even sexualize her erotic vulnerability. Or perhaps she doesn't feel vulnerable at all—she just likes to show off.

Havin' Buck for Breakfast

"Wait, are we going to begin the shot on her penis, then move to his vagina, or vice versa?" The camera guy asked a valid question. "Yes, her penis, then his vagina," responded the director.

You may be slightly confused, but no one on the set of *Allanah*

Starr's Big Boob Adventures was. Last year, I got to sit in on the filming of a scene for the first installment of this transsexual series—a scene that made porn history. It's the first between a male-to-female (MTF) transsexual and a female-to-male transsexual (FTM). And these aren't just any old transsexuals. The she of "her penis" is well-known adult starlet and New York nightlife figure Allanah Starr (www.shemaleexotica.com), and the he of "his vagina" is Buck Angel (www.transexual-man.com), the self-proclaimed "dude with a pussy" and "world's only" FTM porn star.

Buck has been breaking lots of new ground lately. Not only is he the first FTM porn star to run his own membership-based website (which debuted in January 2002), but he's the first to be under contract with a mainstream porn company. In November 2004, he signed a twelve-picture deal to direct and perform for Robert Hill Releasing. The first title as part of that contract, the bisexual *Buck's Beaver,* came out in February 2005, and the feedback has been great, Buck says. "I've heard from lots of people who've said, 'I can't believe it, I have fantasized about guys like you my whole life, I can't believe you really exist.' It's hard to be the only guy like me in porn, but the fan response is really encouraging and helps me keep going."

Boy, is he going. He followed up *Buck's Beaver* with the all-male *More Bang for Your Buck.* But he told me he's been saving himself for a scene with a transsexual woman. Since his deal with Robert Hill is nonexclusive, when the opportunity came to work with Starr, he grabbed it: "Both [director Gia Darling] and Allanah are so great to work with because they are so supportive, and they want me to do well, which means a lot."

Before Angel and his costar got to it, Starr confessed to me that she's had sex with men, women, and transwomen, but never a transman. "I'm excited. We're breaking some taboos," the busty Cuban, who admits she's obsessed with plastic surgery, said. "People know about MTF transsexuals, but some people don't even know that FTMs exist, so we're educating them *and* getting them off."

Directing the scene was performer and director Gia Darling (www.giadarling.com), a groundbreaker herself. An eight-year adult industry veteran, she's the only transsexual woman to own her own production company, and she recently made Starr her first contract performer. I recognized Darling from her appearance on an episode of MTV's plastic surgery show *I Want a Famous Face*— she too is unabashedly in love with cosmetic procedures—but she's known to porn fans for what she calls "her signature soft, romantic, *Playboy*-style tranny videos" of the popular *Transsexual Heart Breakers* series. She admits she is venturing into raunchier territory as director and producer of Starr's new series, although she welcomes the challenge: "Behind most portrayals in tranny porn are men, and there's a lot of 'you dirty-ass whore' this, 'you cum-eating slut' that. When I direct a tranny girl porno, I am representing transsexual women, I am representing myself. I take that seriously."

If you're thinking that everyone's comments here sound more political than those you hear on the set of a typical porn production, you're right. Everyone involved is keenly aware that they are in new, important territory. During the filming of the scene, Starr revealed to Angel that she's a "chick with a dick" (her words) by whipping out her cock from beneath a lacy short skirt. In turn, Angel dropped trou to show her his cunt. The cameraman, who has shot hundreds of skin flicks, was visibly stunned. "Wow," he said as he moved in with his camera to get a closer shot. "Wow. That's a first for me." It was as though he couldn't believe what was right in front of him: a butch, tough, muscled, tattooed guy with a handlebar moustache and a shaved pussy. His eyes adjusted, and he panned over to Starr's cock, by then standing at attention. Without the least bit of sarcasm, he said quietly, "Believe it or not, the universe now makes sense."

It was a simple but profound moment. (You don't get a lot of those on porno sets, folks.) And it was a moment that would not be possible without the courage, exhibitionism, and drive of Buck Angel. He literally lays himself bare so others may better understand some part of transman-ness. There was an unusual collision of fantasy and reality in this production. Darling, Angel, and Starr were not just making jerk-off material or erotic art (or both) as most do when they make porn. This trio, along with a tiny crew, was creating some potentially life-changing images. Somewhere, someone will watch the film and see his transself or his object of affection represented for the first time.

But before I could scream "It's a revolution!" at the top of my lungs, there was work to be done—locating misplaced lube, negotiating how many fingers Buck likes in him, and finding a fucking position that wouldn't kill Starr's knees. Politics or not, there was porn to be made. I couldn't help but notice that Buck bore a strong resemblance to Starr's real-life boyfriend—they're both shortish guys with shaved heads and buff gym bods, although Buck's got lots more tattoos. It was an interesting juxtaposition when the boyfriend would do "fluffer duties" for Starr, and then the cameras would roll again, and she'd be fucking someone who looked like him but with different genitals.

A funny thing happened on the set that day: Not a single person got anyone's pronoun wrong. Not once. Pronouns tend to trip up even the most enlightened folks when it comes to genderqueers, so I was pretty impressed that self-identifications were respected in such a "this is no big deal" way. When Darling wanted something, the directions were clear: "Finger that man!"

Erection Selection

One weekend at a popular club in the meatpacking district, I looked at cock for six hours. I wish I could say I'd snuck into a circle jerk at the Lure, but that infamous leather bar closed its doors in 2004. I, along with adult starlet Carmen Luvana and DJ Whoo Kid from G-Unit and Hot 97, spent the day evaluating the potential of porn star wannabes. Doing our best Simon-Paula-Randy imitations, we assessed the personalities and perused the packages of more than thirty candidates for *Reality-X: The Search for Adam & Eve* (http://searchforadamandeve.com), a new pay-per-view series that premiered in May 2005.

From *The Ozporns* to *Rear Factor*, the adult industry often parodies reality TV, and what's more spoof-worthy than *American Idol*? The most popular show in its genre (more young people voted for the *American Idol* winner than in the last presidential election) has already spawned three full-blown imitations (Platinum X Pictures' *Porn Star Idol*, *Hustler*'s American Porn Idol Contest, and Jet Set's gay *American Porn Star*). Adult giant Adam & Eve launched a multi-city talent search to discover the hottest new couple to fuck on film. Both real couples and single people who don't mind being paired with an unknown partner are eligible to audition. Sixteen semifinalists were flown to Jamaica to compete for a chance to star in a movie and win a contract with Adam & Eve worth up to $250,000.

During the course of our cock 'n' cunt critique, it was no surprise to me that we saw two couples, one single woman, and about twenty-five single men. More men than women aspire to be video fuck studs for hire, all of them believe they've got what it takes, and most think all they have to do is bone hot girls for a living. There's a reason why there are hundreds of women in porn, yet you see the same handful of guys in every movie: It's one of the toughest jobs around. A male porn star has to get hard on command and stay hard for an unnaturally long time. He has to fuck in the cold outdoors, fuck when he's not turned on, and fuck when another guy is holding a hot light an inch away from his ass. The straight male porn star is an underpaid, unsung hero who has uncanny abilities. And he's hard to find.

We asked contestants questions like: What's the wildest sexual thing you've ever done? (Favorite answer, delivered with most bravado: "I don't want to go into too much detail, but I will say it involved strawberries and whipped cream!") And: What qualifies you to be the next great porn star? ("I just got an audition to be an extra on *Third Watch,* so my career is really going places.") Then we invited them to show us their best attributes, and this part of the process involved guys performing a spontaneous striptease, while DJ Whoo Kid checked e-mail on his Blackberry. Carmen, taking a cue from Miss Abdul's upbeat and ever so gracious attitude, even talked dirty and showed her tits to some for encouragement. But this is where the reality of XXX reality TV came into play: Could these guys get it up on a set full of bright lights, multiple cameras, and a crew of forty (mostly male) onlookers? An intimidating situation to be sure, but a simulation of what it's like on a porn set.

A twentysomething dude from Boston announced proudly, "I have huge balls." I've never heard any guy use that as a selling point before. (I asked a gay male friend if that would appeal to him, and he shrugged, "They're just like big boobs on a girl, fun to play with, I guess.") He did, in fact, have very large and low-hanging cojones, and he also smacked his own ass as he worked his tool. I just kept thinking about this one popular shot where the camera is underneath the copulating couple, and how this guy's balls would obscure her pussy in that shot; that could be a liability. One guy told us that if he broke into the business, he'd like to use his childhood nickname, which people still call him: the Garanimal. I explained to him that Garanimals is a children's clothing line with little animals on the tops and bottoms, and while it may convey "Look, Mom! I can match my clothes myself!" it doesn't actually say "blue-movie hunk."

We asked another guy to act out a student–teacher role-play fantasy with Carmen. He immediately named himself Professor Lance, and told her that in order to bring her grades up, she'd have to get Mr. Lance up. "That's how it is in the school of hard cocks," he said, without even cracking a smile. In the next audition, a genuine nerd—who looked like the ultimate scrawny, mild-mannered, dorky accountant—said he could get a boner anytime, anywhere. I turned my head to say something to Carmen, and when I looked back, sure enough, it was standing at attention. It was by far the fastest erection achieved and one of the more solid ones we'd seen all day. My advice to him: "You gotta work your geeky guy thing. Don't listen to anyone who tells you to get contacts or go to the gym. Embrace who you are."

We met bartenders, cabdrivers, former stockbrokers, and a hot rocker guy with a big Delaware belt buckle and the best-looking cock of the bunch. We saw a former competitive gymnast and a New York Golden Gloves boxing champ. But it ultimately became a blur of mostly flaccid cocks and earnest guys struggling to get them up. Worse than their performance anxiety (which I sympathize with) was that too many were just plain dull. I'd like to think I'm not the only girl in the world who wants some personality to go with a penis.

My favorite couple was a perky, petite, uninhibited blonde with beautiful natural breasts and a cute ass and her boyfriend, a thick, muscular, tall guy who looked twice her size. She called the shots, telling him what to do and how to do it. It's that kind of take-charge attitude coupled with her comfort with her sexuality that could serve her well in the adult industry. They're headed to Jamaica, and while I guarantee they will go all the way, I hope they win too.

The Art of Anal Fisting

"Anal fisting: party trick or real sex act?" A writer once posed this question to me during an interview. I giggled, but he did have a point. Most people think anal fisting is either a gay urban legend or a freakish sexual circus feat. Actually, it can be a real sex act and a party trick, if you play your cards right and know what you're doing.

So where does one learn the art of anal fisting? In Florida, of course. Several years ago, the Hollywood Clarion Hotel, just outside Fort Lauderdale, was the site of one of the few national events of the S/M community: "Living in Leather." This was the 14th annual conference of the National Leather Association International, an umbrella organization for ten city or state chapters devoted to S/M politics, education, and social events. (There's an affiliate in Calgary, hence NLAI's international scope.) The weekend at the Clarion offered S/M seminar staples: workshops, meetings, shopping, awards, and play parties. As a professional known as Buttgirl, I had the honor of teaching two workshops this year: Anal Toys 101 and Anal Fisting.

Now, when I say the words *anal fisting,* most people's immediate reaction is a wide-eyed, half terrified, half titillated "Yikes!" Take a deep breath. (It's all in the breathing.) Anal fisting, also known as handballing, is the gradual process of putting your hand (and for very experienced players, sometimes your forearm) inside someone's ass. *Fisting* as a term is misleading since you don't go inside all at once like a punch; usually your hand is not in a clenched fist once it is in there. Gay men popularized fisting in the late '60s and '70s during the sexual revolution and founded private fisting clubs in major urban areas.

I've read and heard tales of these sex clubs, filled with hungry men, waiting slings, and cans of Crisco. Although it is an intense exchange of power between two people, fisting isn't exactly S/M. Because it is an outlaw sexual practice popularized by gay leathermen, it remains associated with and practiced by S/M folk, although not exclusively. Yet like S/M, anal fisting explores and tests the farthest reaches of the mind's and body's inner limits.

Anal fisting is a rarity among women, even though vaginal fisting has been somewhat accepted. The vagina has long demonstrated its versatility, but sexual adventurers have paid so much attention to this one fabulously flexible orifice that they have overlooked the promise of the other. As a result, unlike gay men, women lack a history to hang on to like a sturdy sling, the legacy of fisting pros, or the role models to pass the skills from generation to generation.

I was scheduled to teach the anal-fisting class with leatherman and leading handball expert Bert Herrman, author of the only book devoted exclusively to the subject, *Trust: The Hand Book*. He also publishes *Trust: The Handballing Newsletter*. Bert, a fisting legend, has been putting his hands in men's asses since I was in diapers. A true meeting of the minds and asses, the workshop in Florida proved to be a unique bridging of different perspectives, genders, and generations. In our introduction, when we talked about warming up for fisting, our differences were readily apparent. An old-school fister, Bert's into getting high on pot and poppers and stuffing gobs of Crisco, whereas I am into endorphin highs and a nice, thick water-based lubricant.

We viewed *Handball Loving*, which is unlike any video I've

ever seen. Bert's approach to fisting is very spiritual; he sees it as a path to enlightenment and higher consciousness, a way to connect with a higher power and soul-bond with another person. He draws on Eastern religions, particularly the principles of Tantric sex. In that way, he is at the forefront of future sex, incorporating spirituality into sexuality.

Then there is the simple amazement factor of seeing Bert with his arm almost to the elbow up his partner's ass, then later with both hands inside him. It really is a different kind of sex; yes, there's pleasure and intimacy and orgasm, but that's not all. Both men were transported into a deep trance, their bodies melding, their souls merging.

That night, after the workshop, I was inspired. I've been anally fisted before, but it was a long time ago and I wanted to do it again. My girlfriend, Red, and I had already decided to host a small sex party, a half-dozen of us, in our room. I started with a medium-sized butt plug (appropriately called Voyager) in my ass, which I wore for a while, then switched to a larger, very thick red plug. Whenever that one slides in my ass, it feels too big at first, but inevitably I take a deep breath and in it goes.

When I felt that my ass was relaxed and ready for more, Red put on a latex glove, slipped out the butt plug, and started working her fingers inside me as I lay on my back. I took lots of deep breaths and concentrated on relaxing and opening up. She eventually got all five fingers up to the final knuckles—the widest part of the hand, the dreaded sticking point. Totally turned-on, totally amazed that there was so much of her in my ass, I tried to flip over on my stomach. "Whoa, whoa," Red insisted. I was so absorbed I didn't realize I would've broken her arm if I continued to roll. I kept asking for more lube, but finally Red said, "Honey, you have a ton of lube in your ass. There's just no more room."

We both knew this was as far as she was going. At this point, an orgasm doesn't matter, because the experience is physically and mentally so intense and all encompassing. Red withdrew and we relaxed. We then enjoyed some cheese and crackers with our guests.

During the scene, I remembered Bert talking about what it feels like when you're all the way up to someone's transverse colon (beyond the rectum and descending colon). I realized I'm definitely a below-the-transverse-colon person. Even Buttgirl has her limits.

An Ode to Ass

One look at this year's best-selling porn titles and the trend is clear: When folks have a choice of threesomes, interracial sex, amateurs, eighteen-year-olds, MILFs, and nearly every other sexual niche imaginable, they choose anal-themed movies. And it's not just pornophiles either. From men's magazines to self-help books, anal sex is always high on the list of people's fantasies. It's one of the most frequently searched-for terms on the Web. So what is it about behinds and banging them that gets us so hot and bothered? I've got a few theories.

The ass has been eroticized for centuries. We can all agree that a butt's something to check out as it walks by in tight jeans, pat gently in admiration, squeeze on the sly, cup firmly when you've got a mouthful of pussy or cock, or dig your heels into while you're getting fucked. Between the cheeks, there's a whole lot more going on. The idea of the ass as an erogenous zone in its own right is not new, but the public discussion of it is.

For such a tight-lipped little area, the butthole says a whole lot about American culture. With nicknames ranging from flowery (rosebud) to filthy (poop chute), the brown eye is full of complexity and contradiction. It represents strength and control to some and ultimate vulnerability to others. It's delicate yet resilient, and embodies some of our deepest needs—things like privacy, trust, and power. Some fear it, others fetishize it, and everyone has to think about it on a regular basis. Talk of it can elicit feelings from stress to silliness. What other hole do you know that is associated with Freudian pathology, puritanical repression, and homophobia? That's one busy orifice.

While it symbolizes some of our fundamental fixations, it transcends another of our collective obsessions: gender. In this age of gender fluidity and transgendered bodies, the ass emerges as a kind of neutral territory of the flesh. While genderqueers attempt to reimagine, reclaim, and even rename sites of pleasure like breasts, cunts, and cocks that are heavily identified as male or female, the ass is everyman's hole—a source of pleasure unencumbered by society's expectations.

Why we fantasize about anal sex reveals just how powerful and varied its meanings are. To lots of people, anal sex is unattainable in a no-means-you-are-never-ever-going-there-honey kind of way. We want it because it's out of our reach. It turns us on like banging the boss's hot wife, doing Angelina Jolie, or having a threesome with them both—precisely because it ain't gonna happen.

In addition to wanting what we can't have, we're also aroused by what we're not supposed to do—the thing that would shock our friends and neighbors at church if they found out we did it. We like to misbehave, especially when it comes to sex. Anal sex fulfills our desire to be the sexual rebel, to stray from convention, to be, quite simply, naughty.

Assfucking does not just challenge societal norms; it can also be a way to test the limits of the body. You can ask an awful lot of a very small opening. (Think anal fisting up to the elbow.) Those limits are one of the most popular subjects of the letters I receive, with questions like: How wide is too wide? How long can a toy be? How much can I fit in my ass? Some people don't necessarily want to actually do it, but they want to fantasize about doing it or watch someone else do it. Gaping—where, after lots of penetration, the anus is wide open—is increasingly popular in anal sex videos and is a good example of imagery that affirmingly depicts how far our bodies can go.

When all you hear is dick–pussy this and dick–pussy that, the ass remains neglected and overlooked, but this oversight contributes to its mysterious quality. That *Star Trek* fan in all of us is excited by the element of darkness, the unknown, the mystique of a place where no one has gone before. It's our frontier-exploring, cowboy spirit that yearns to make the tough journey, then plant our flagpole to mark our territory.

It's no secret I love anal sex, in real life and on video. (Yes, I admit I fast-forward straight to the buttfucking.) For me, it's all about power and consciousness. I think that every sexual exchange is a power exchange and playing with that dynamic is what can make sex extraordinary. Anal sex is the perfect vehicle for dominance and submission play since so much of it is about control and surrender. Because of the way it has been represented (often as violent) and the fact that you could actually hurt someone if you don't do it right, there is a sense of danger.

On top of that, it's not exactly something most people can just do. Very few performers can phone in an anal scene in a video, and nonprofessionals need time, preparation, and a whole lot more for it to work. That's why, in videos, the players' self-awareness seems more palpable to me during anal sex. It's as if you can see everyone's brain working: The receiver is thinking, *Breathe, pace yourself, get to that place where it's gonna work*, and the giver is thinking, *How fast can I go? I want to get this right*. They are really engaged with their own bodies and with one another.

The growing popularity of that puckered hole and where it leads is undeniable. Anal sex represents the ultimate collision between public and private: A person gets to go inside another's deepest, darkest place, to feel it and to know it through an erotic act laced with cultural taboos (more so than other acts). In Hollywood movies, buttfucking is still most often shown as degrading; in some gay-male fisting videos, it's portrayed as a transformative experience. In porn, it seems that there's some of both, mirroring the capacity of anal sex to be represented, imagined, and experienced as intense violation, stunning revelation, or something else entirely.

What I'm Giving Up
Mark Pritchard

In the afterword to my erotic short story collection *Too Beautiful and Other Stories,* I told readers that if they lived far from a large city and wanted to live out their sexual fantasies, they had two choices: start their own scene or move someplace like San Francisco, where, I wrote, there really are people like the polyamorous, polysexual characters I depicted in my stories. There really are sex parties here; there really are S/M lesbians, orgiastic gay male sex bashes, experimentally minded bisexuals, couples who live in Daddy/boy arrangements, and so on.

I gained my real initiation into this sexual demimonde as so many have: I became a San Francisco Sex Information phone volunteer. At the same time, 1990, I started my magazine *Frighten the Horses,* and I joined Queer Nation. Suddenly I was part of a network of creative sexual revolutionaries. I met strippers who did performance art, sex writers who worked in galleries, prostitutes with zines or rock bands, polyamorist activist Ph.D. students, and painters who bought art supplies with the money they earned lap dancing on weekends.

Among these cheerfully transgressive youths was a woman in her mid-twenties, Stephanie. I met her in Queer Nation's bisexual affinity group, and when I learned she was a comix artist I asked her to do some illustrations for *Frighten the Horses*. So it was through this connection that, after knowing each other for a few years, we became lovers.

While Stephanie and I were going through the same getting-to-know-you flirtations that all lovers do, I found out that, in addition to her comix artwork, she was a dancer at the Lusty Lady strip club. I didn't want to come off like a typical slobbering male, so without actually saying so I tried to make the conversation sound more like I was conducting research. I asked respectful, sympathetic questions about hours and working conditions, the relationship between workers and management, the ins and outs of working in the "booth" where dancers had one-on-one encounters (albeit still separated by Plexiglas) with customers.

Of course, behind my polite facade, I wanted to know what any man wants to know about a stripper's job: Is it a turn-on, or is it just like any job where you feign interest for the customer's sake? Is it interesting or even arousing when men masturbate in response to a dancer, or is it merely objectionable and gross? And most important of all, is there any reality to the pornographic stereotype that the girls turn each other on and have hot girl-on-girl action in the locker room?

I wanted to know all those things, but I didn't have the nerve to ask them at first. It took quite a while before I finally satisfied my curiosity about the ins and outs of working at the Lusty. By then, we had been lovers for months. If I arrived early at the theater to pick up Stephanie at the end of her shift, I walked around mingling with the customers but reveling in the secret knowledge that I was not one of them. I wasn't *just* a customer; I was getting what they only fantasized about. Listening to Stephanie talk about work, I came to share her perspective, and her coworkers', that the customers were more or less to be looked down on, or at least pitied. In our intimate conversations, and once at an offsite spoken-word performance organized by the dancers, I laughed with them at the customers' foibles, at the gulf between the customers' stereotypical fantasies and their schlubby reality.

The most flattering confirmation of the difference between them and me came one day when I was, as usual, early to pick up Stephanie. I wandered into the one-on-one booth and put a twenty into the slot. I didn't say anything about being a dancer's boyfriend; I just began talking to the performer as if I were making small talk at a party instead of talking to a naked chick under glass. After making sure that I really wasn't there to jack off, she relaxed and just started chatting with me. After a few minutes she said, "You don't seem like a regular customer," and then I admitted that I was, in fact, in the boyfriend category.

Only after several years can I see the irony of this situation. Secure in the knowledge that I was somehow different from—even better than—the men who were the run-of-the-mill customers, I presented myself as different. The performer, in response, treated me exactly as she would have any other customer: She confirmed and reflected what she assumed was my fantasy. And I had, in fact, paid her to do this. So by attempting to set myself apart from and above the louche customers, I had done nothing more than become one.

Though I learned that it was not true, of course, that the dancers had pornographic interactions in the locker room, they did have relationships of various types outside the club. The spoken-word evening that I mentioned above was only one example. They'd go to dance clubs or the Folsom Street Fair or twelve-step meetings together; they went to each other's art openings, perfor-mances, and readings. Stephanie told me of one occasion when, to celebrate a dancer's birthday, several of them went to a local sex club; there they jokingly bossed around the birthday girl, who was known to be submissive, making her perform erotic chores. Most of the dancers were lesbian or bisexual; a few were lovers. Stephanie had an on-and-off affair with a woman who worked at a massage parlor; I'd introduced them, and on two memorable oc-casions the three of us went to bed together.

Stephanie was a perfect lover. She was generous with her affec-tions to the point of self-denial; she was experimental and willing to do anything I proposed. When I told her, early in our affair, that getting a blow job had never been my favorite way to come, she took that as a challenge. We did S/M; we did role-playing; we went to sex parties together; we had sex on drugs; we had threesomes. She never said no, and she came up with plenty of ideas of her own.

This, one of the momentous affairs of my life, took place almost ten years ago. It's taken me that long to figure out how to write about it. Part of the problem is that it's hard to say something origi-nal about having a hot affair with a bisexual stripper, which every man fantasizes about. So when I say, for example, that we had a threesome with one of her coworkers, I want to tell you about the parts of the experience that set it apart from fantasy—the odd bits, the parts that didn't work, the moments of awkwardness.

"There's a girl at work," Stephanie told me one day. "She's a dyke, but she said once in a while she feels like getting fucked by a real prick. I told her I was with someone who was cool and would respect her boundaries. Do you want to do it?"

Did I want to do a threesome with two bisexual San Francisco strippers? Well, sure I did. But while my first reaction was to grab Stephanie by her shoulders and shout, "When?! Where?! Can we do it right now?!" I sensed that if I acted too eager I might not be considered cool enough to participate at all. It's the old rule: If you want someone, act as if you don't.

So I said, "Oh…. Sure…. Sounds like fun. Yeah, sure."

Typically for modern San Francisco, it took us a few weeks to iron out everybody's schedule. During this time Stephanie would check in with me about a certain date, and I would answer back in the laconic voice I'd chosen for this particular interaction. I was so successful in maintaining my cool that she even asked me if I really wanted to do it, so I had to assure her I did, still maintaining my cool all the while. Eventually it was arranged, and we finally got together one evening, picking the girl up after an evening class at San Francisco State and driving back across town to Stephanie's apartment in the Tenderloin. Before going upstairs to the apartment, we stopped in a bar to negotiate our encounter, since the girl's lover had put certain limits on what she could do. She could fuck me—that was the whole point—but not kiss me. She'd go down on me, but I wasn't allowed to go down on her.

Finally we went upstairs and fucked, and the best moment was when I penetrated her and she exclaimed, "It's so warm!" because she was accustomed to silicone and plastic. Though I had to keep myself in line, Stephanie had had no limits imposed on her. She fisted the girl while I watched.

Did my affair with Stephanie make me happy? Of course—we did everything I'd ever wanted to. There were many times I reminded myself to cherish our time together, because I sensed it wouldn't last forever. But it did last a long time. Each of us plumbed the depths of our desire, coming up with new positions, new partners, new places to fuck, new fantasies to enact.

But after a few years, we'd done everything we could think of, and then what do you do? What do you do when all your sexual fantasies have been fulfilled, when there are no more barriers to push through, no more taboos to transgress? The answer is, you do the things that you don't particularly want to do, but because everyone else talks about them, you do them. It may surprise you to find that, in our case, this was nothing more exotic than butt-fucking.

Anal sex is a practice about which I'm sort of neutral and something Stephanie had never learned to appreciate, so we had never gone there. But in the last months of our affair—when, as in any long-term relationship, the little annoying things, the unresolved arguments and hurt feelings, were mounting up, making it harder to be together—she seized on the idea that things weren't going well because she hadn't broken through this particular barrier. So she insisted that we try. As usual when neither person really wants to do something, the result was a failure: Anxious minutes of grappling with lube, towels, and each other, with her trying to ease herself backwards onto my cock and me asking, "Look, are you sure you want to do this?" until she would give up and collapse onto the bed in tears. We repeated this scene at least three times in as many weeks until dropping the whole subject. And the worst part was that, after all the crazy outré stuff we'd done together, this failed attempt at assfucking—the act that neither of us really wanted to do—was the first time we were actually embarrassed.

The other thing about getting to a far point with a lover is that you tend to take for granted all the great stuff you did on the way there. At least I took her affections for granted—I think she never presumed mine. When we broke up after four years, she told me,

with great bitterness, "You don't know what you're giving up."
Two years later, she died in a highway accident.

In the end, she was right. Only since our breakup have I come to know what I'm missing. Because while this is San Francisco, and there are still plenty of artistic, polyamorous bisexual people around, I'm now in my late forties, and all those youngsters are with each other.

I still visit the Lusty Lady from time to time, partly to keep in touch with that memorable affair, but also because it's one of the few places where I can go and talk to someone like Stephanie— someone sexually open, willing to participate in any fantasy. But now I am, like everyone else, just a customer.

Good Fences Make Good Affairs
Virginia Vitzthum

I knew it was a setup—thank you again, Pat—but Josh did not. His bright blue-gray eyes drew me immediately, but turned away from mine. We spent the party talking in groups, and though he didn't say much, he mocked, amusingly, a movie I hated too. I mistook that scorn for confidence and told Pat so on our drive home. I said I was interested but wasn't sure he was. She said, "No, no, he's shy. He was sneaking looks at you all night."

He went away for the summer and I forgot about him. When he came back, he had shed his beard and about twenty pounds. He was delectable. I invited him to a Friday-night art opening, for which I primped extravagantly. When he finally strode in, I coolly bounded over. Our eyes were darting and our chat was coded: He wanted to get me alone too! I had to duck a second, less exciting prospect whom I had also invited to the opening, just in case. Josh and I slipped out of the gallery and went, for some reason, to a movie starring Marcello Mastroianni and a dwarf.

I think the movie was terrible, but in all fairness, I was focused on the few inches between our bare arms, and on the pace of his breathing. I twisted in my seat a few times to give Josh a better view of my breasts, fluffed for his delectation with my new Wonderbra. Finally, "Fine," and we reentered the warm night, close but not touching. I offered him a ride to his car. As soon as the car doors closed, our mouths glided together as if they were on a track. He kissed wonderingly, lips inching over lips' curves, like someone discovering a charming new custom. Then he turned expert, teasing with hints of tongue. Little groans and yelps steamed up the windows; I squirmed on the seat.

Josh, who was generally shy, surprised me pleasantly by suggesting we repair somewhere. We sped both cars to my house, and pawed each other on the way in the door. I got under the covers and watched him undress. He had long muscled thighs, small hips and waist, and a short weight lifter's torso. His skin was clear and white. His erection ran straight up past his belly button, a thick red tree against a marble wall. His naked body was a thing of beauty, but not the contemplative kind. Not with that red wood glistening in the candlelight.

Before I could answer his body's call to action, however, there was shame to navigate. Not Garden-of-Eden shame but the kind you buy in magazines. The superpowers of the Wonderbra lay on the floor somewhere, and I began panicking that this visual artist, this aesthete with the body of a sculpture would just leave when he saw me naked. Part of me (inconveniently, not the cellulite) floated off into fear and self-loathing. Josh drew me back to the present as if he could read my mind. He slowly pulled the sheets off like wrapping paper and made me beautiful, fanning his eyes, tongue, fingers, skin over all of me, studying every reverberation of his touch on my body like a safecracker. I started grabbing for him, twisting my hips up helplessly, but he went at his own exquisite pace of leisurely urgency. I-can't-wait ran simultaneous with all the time in the world. He kept stirring me for hours, Tantric pace stretched unbearably taut till we snapped into lamp-knocking-over and neighbor-waking. Then stunned rest, hearts banging against each other slower and slower. We fell asleep just before dawn still entwined, which was rare enough for this fussy light sleeper to read as a portent.

I stuffed myself at the diner the next morning and lolled on him like a cat. I telegraphed "not a one-night stand" in our parting kiss, willing my mouth to express without words as well as his did. I floated through the weekend: I'd struck a mother lode of sex, and love was not ruled out. My two major affairs of the heart had begun with nights less satisfying.

The First Fence

He didn't call all week. I didn't yield to despair till Thursday, and Friday night I spent four grim hours at the gym, a full-scale assault on the thigh fat I knew had driven him away. I disregarded all my strategic advisers and called him in a tizzy on Saturday. I demanded to know if he wanted to date me or what. It had, after all, been a week.

He was so taken aback he wasn't even defensive. He hadn't called because he'd been devising a way to cast molds. He explained at great length his solution to this artistic hurdle, inviting me to share in his excitement. A great gulf appeared: I assumed he'd been thinking about me all week too, even if it was to decide I was too repulsive to call. But he'd been melting plastic. I pressed again for intentions. He said, "Look, can we talk about this in person? Can I see you?"

We met a few nights later in a crowded café. We chit-chatted, then opened discussions. To my grilling, Josh whined, "I don't know. What do YOU want?" It seemed he was withdrawing, that he was not mine to lose, so I told the truth. "I'd like to mate for life and have kids. How about you?"

He ignored my declaration and began explaining himself, his voice rising in frustration. "Maybe it sounds ridiculous, but I want to make it as an artist. That's all I know I want. I don't know if I want to be involved with anyone. I don't own a house; I don't have any money; I'm like an eighteen-year-old kid. Look at me," he finished incongruously. "I'm thirty-five, and I've got a ponytail."

I looked, as instructed, at Josh's ponytail, light brown curls resting on his shoulders, which sloped, sturdy as furniture, into his collarbones, then his neck. He had just shaved. His mouth turned down at the corners, a little haughty, and his upper lip had an extra set of curves. I noticed for the first time how his tongue was visible in the tiny gap between his front teeth. I remembered how he tasted sweet and uncorrupted—he didn't smoke and barely drank. His lips had been so smooth. I was so lost gazing at his mouth that I had no idea if it was still telling me to take my grown-up needs elsewhere. When his voice reentered my consciousness, the defensive whine was gone. All husky, it was saying, "Let's get out of here."

We left the conversation in the café and stumbled down the street, our arms wound around each other somehow. "Those girls were laughing at me. Come in here," he said, pulling me into a doorway. "Why were they laughing?" I asked, trying to follow the curiouser and curiouser turns in the evening. He pointed down to the prow of his pants. "My fault?" I laughed. He dragged my hips slowly up the prow and licked my neck. Again, we raced two cars back to my house.

We never referred again to the talk in the café, and soon we were sleeping together two or three times a week. He'd built the first fence, though, and I quickly followed suit. I renamed what I felt: Not love, but lust.

I swaggered through my doubts when I told my friends about this amazing lay. "Serious? It's way too much fun to be serious." The relief was as genuine as the disappointment: The confines of the physical are more navigable than love's tangle and sprawl. And the sex is more transcendent: Only uncomplicated orgasms take you out of yourself. Within an evolving relationship, sex becomes a workhorse weighed down with obscure communications and agendas.

The Sex Zone Grows

Josh focused completely on the moment, which was wonderful in bed, less so when he spent days in the darkroom not calling. Other things bothered me too: He complained and overexplained. I loved his art and said so frequently, but he still bragged about his credentials. Out in the world he was tentative and resentful.

In bed, though, he self-actualized like Oz bursting into color. More sides of him unfolded: relaxed, in charge, nurturing. He became more specific, more happy, more responsive, more connected to me. He made love and art more expressively than he spoke. Josh taught me the meaning of the expression "fuck her brains out." It had always sounded so hostile, but now I understood the appeal of jettisoning some ego that way. Josh took me out past language, where I could only gibber like a monkey or a Pentecostal. I was happy to be fucked so deep into sensation, so out of my head.

I was thirty-four, and Josh was the Sherpa for my sexual peak. He found new heights of sensation and response in my body. After years of too-sensitive irritability, my nipples suddenly become almost orgasmic, as if the wiring had finally been uncrossed. One afternoon, bored at work, a fantasy about sucking Josh's cock popped into my head. I'd never even particularly liked doing that, especially with one as huge as Josh's, and suddenly here I was desiring it in the abstract.

It was the perfect time for a vacation from analyzing, assessing, arguing. I'd recently had my heart broken by a writer who had withdrawn sexually, blaming depression and its chemical cures. He managed, however, to rustle up the serotonin to screw a few women behind my back. Tongue-tied, priapic Josh was the perfect antidote to this wordy weasel, and I was salve for his wounds too. My predecessor was a dour artist who found saliva and jism icky and had confined Josh to a few dry behaviors. This seemed to me like telling Shakespeare to go ahead and write, but only limericks.

Our sex room kept growing, like Max's in *Where the Wild Things Are*. Josh was strong enough to hoist me up and screw me against the wall. His power made me feel perfectly feminine— small, pretty, claimed—and I restored to him the confidence stolen by his ex, the Carrie Nation of body fluids. Our male and female selves thus secured, we began to wander into each other's territory. I would push him down and tear his clothes off to straddle him or to slide first my fingers, then a strap-on dildo, into his asshole. It was the first time I'd enjoyed watching parts of me disappear inside someone else. And he loved being desired and taken, and the trust bound us further.

We made room for performance—the few extra decibels or shudders that heighten sex for actor and costar/audience. Some playacting can't survive everyday intimacy: Most of my sex experiments with serious boyfriends were abandoned amid embarrassed laughter. Absent any talk of a future, sex with Josh got more inventive. We seemed less like individuals and more like archetypes or people playing with archetypes.

One winter night, Josh's beauty woke up the sleeping objectifier in me. We'd been to a party in my neighborhood. Meeting people made him nervous, and on the way in, he had a little panic attack and asked me to stick close by him. We left earlier than I wanted to. His confidence returned when we got to his power spot, the bedroom, and he soon had me out of my party dress. But I was tired, menstruating, a little irritated, and I didn't want the usual lavish attentions. I'd done our performing at the party; now I wanted to watch. I asked Josh to masturbate for me. He warmed up to it quickly, keeping his eyes down. I'd move in occasionally to lick his nipple or his ear, but mostly I just watched, another first. I was a little appalled at how turned on I was, waiting for the money shot like some perv quivering in his raincoat.

To the Limits

Josh allowed me to slip into the straightforward sexuality of men. Whenever my girlfriends would complain "men are so predictable" or "they all want the same thing," I'd say, "Praise be!" I love the joy men take in simple things that we can provide—an ass up in the air, hot breath in their ear, simply coordinating the hand and the mouth. I'd hate to have to seduce women, with our need for narrative and emotional context and the strange hooded mysteries of our orgasms. People are complicated enough; why can't sex be a refuge of simplicity?

Because it's not. Sex is something that does not love a wall. Lying in the dark with Josh, floating back to earth, I wanted more and more for us to share a language, to need less translation than other people. Happy though my orifices were, I needed more receptors filled. I needed more because the heat of the sex perversely promised more and because the coldness of my objectifying was starting to scare me.

By February, I couldn't deny the familiar three-to-six-month fork in the road. If we, if I, didn't fall in love soon, this relationship would be Woody Allen's dead shark. But the sex has never been this brilliant, I protested to my heart, and I don't want to give it up. I threw myself into more fucking, more experiments.

But I had to admit that what sex was transporting me from was a guy I didn't love talking with. I admired Josh's visual and physical acuity and he was smart, but I craved wit and nuance and word-play and ideas built together. I wanted surprise and yet familiarity. I wanted to be learning new things about being human. I wanted intimacy.

My silence about the relationship, meanwhile, endeared me to Josh, who assumed we were doing great. He was shocked when I broke it off in the car five months after we'd met, driving home from *The Cook, The Thief, His Wife, and Her Lover*. The words had been bubbling in me, and Greenaway's shallow voluptuousness got me queasy enough to spit them out. Josh protested the breakup and made some weak declarations that didn't include the word *love* or the future.

Four weeks later, I crawled back to his house on the pretense of returning a jacket and apologetically threw myself at him. He backed away, narrowed his pretty eyes, and said, "You know, I asked myself all day, *Did she just call because she's horny?*" He had correctly surmised that I was thinking from below, but my pussy was a bit less sly than most dicks facing such a question. I answered, "The two are not entirely unrelated."

He didn't laugh. He described the pain the breakup caused him, the extent of which surprised him. I wasn't that shocked—I knew he was lucky to find a woman who could heat up sexually and not demand some kind of pledge. I knew most women would have wanted more. I knew we were enjoying something rare: a spacious arrangement with someone decent, not crazy, likable, and a great sexual fit.

The Perfect Wall

Dammit, there was compatibility there. Fuck the words, fuck the fork, fuck the shark. I groveled and apologized, and then we went upstairs to hammer away at some new arrangement, some new sex shack built just for us, outside the normal categories of relationship. My body celebrated our reunion, but hopelessness rumbled underneath. I knew we'd just replay the trip up to the fork and then break up again. Maybe a few times, each less fun, with generosity dwindling and emotional windows closing.

But I'm a slow learner. I lather, rinse, repeat with men less sexy and nice than Josh, and I knew I'd do it again. Driving east from his house the next day, I mourned preemptively for the best that had already passed and for its dull echo that lay ahead, fading over the next months to nothing.

Then, suddenly, a gift from fate. Josh was offered a job overseas. It was a great job, he was happy, he was leaving in June. Just like that, time was on our side, and our supply of affection no longer dwindling. With the end in sight, our hearts were free to roam alongside our bodies.

I made him tapes of love songs and he printed and framed his photographs to decorate my house. I helped him pack and pick up the U-Haul and move furniture into storage. We studied maps of his new city together; I edited his artist's statement.

I finally referred to him as my boyfriend that spring. No future made us an ideal present. And now the best sex I ever had exists in past perfect.

Just Always Be Good
Stephen Elliott

The first thing Eden does is take my clothes off and tie me up. She uses a long black rope, starts with my balls and my penis, continues to my ankles, then from my wrists to my ankles, all of it a series of complicated knots. She wraps a collar around my neck and ties the rope to the collar, so that almost any movement pulls on my genitals. I'm going to New York tomorrow. We're not going to see each other for twelve days.

I'm on the hardwood floor of my bedroom, on my back. I can put my feet down or my head, but not both. She pushes me and I fall on my side. I've been tied up many times, but everything is different with Eden.

I once followed a woman into her apartment on the Upper West Side. There were piles of stuffed animals as high as our knees. The animals spilled onto the mattress, which was uncovered. The walls were smeared in red graffiti. There was a dog leashed to an open refrigerator. I realized when it was too late that I had followed a crazy person home. She tied my arms over my head, blindfolded me, burned me all over my body with her cigarette. That's the kind of thing I used to do before Eden. I'd go home with anybody; I just wanted to be hurt. I have scars.

This is the opposite of that. This is a happy story.

Eden cradles my head in her lap, her bag nearby. Yesterday her mother had a biopsy. There was a chance Eden wasn't going to be able to come over today, depending on how things went. Eden has thick thighs, comfortable legs. I'm so far gone, so in love, I can barely think. I stare at her cheeks, her nose. I can see every pore, blood vessels below the surface of her skin, hairs that will turn gray one day.

Eden attaches a clip to my nipple. "Do you want another one?" she asks. "Yes, please," I say. And that's how it goes, as my voice gets weaker and she lines my body with her clips, finally running a string of them down my penis. Every movement increases the pain.

"You're being so good," she says.

"I love you so much," I whisper back.

She strokes my face. I keep thinking to myself how nice she is, wondering why she is so nice to me. It makes me want to cry. We have the whole day. Her husband said she could spend the night; her son is away at camp. My roommate is home, in the next room, with his music turned up. That's the world around us. And then there is Eden and I and all the clips she's decorated me with, her initials carved across my back, the bruises on my belly, the twenty-five stripes she cut into my shoulders.

"So pretty," she says.

She takes the clips off one at a time. We've been together over five weeks now. I see her four or five days a week, sometimes more, sometimes less. We don't always do this. We go to movies. We go dancing. We shop for fabric and groceries and I keep her company while she sews. I go to her house and I make her breakfast and sit on the floor next to her chair, working on my articles, while she manages her affairs, her husband at work in the city. We do other things, but this is what we're doing now.

I try to breathe deeply as she removes the clips. The clips on my penis hurt so much. I've made it much worse with small movements. It's hard for me to stay still. "Oh, god," I say when she pulls the clips from my penis in one motion, tugging the rope, like a zipper. Everything is white for a second. There's this sound I'm making and I'm in the back of my head watching myself. "Come back to me," I hear. It's a voice so far away.

When my vision returns, Eden is there. "Hi," she says. She's smiling. "You took a lot." I try to respond, say anything. I want to tell her that I once rode a bus late at night when I was thirteen. Everything was purple and yellow. The acid was so strong at four in the morning I thought the police officer was Napoleon. My friend's father picked us up when the sun came out and he took my friend home and I walked down Devon Avenue into Little India and scaled a drainpipe onto a roof and slept the morning covered in cardboard boxes. I want to tell her that when I was in fifth grade I was so good at dodgeball I was the best in my class. I played soccer, chess. I want to brag, stand on my hands. I want to impress her.

But she keeps her eyes on me and I don't say anything. She pulls a bar from her pocket, slides a square of chocolate between my lips, and I start to cry.

I'm still lying on the hard floor when Eden suggests untying me. "No," I say. "Please." I'm worried that I'll cry and she'll stop. When I've been with women and cried before, they always stopped. I don't want her to stop. I don't want her to go. So she

holds me for a while and then slides out from under me, rolling me
onto my side, pressing her hand across my face.

She hits me first on my left cheek. She's still smiling but my
vision is going again. I'm crawling into my head, tucking into that
little room. I have no right to be here. I have never done anything
to deserve someone like Eden. The slaps get harder, and then the
other side. I'm not in the same place anymore. I try to see Eden
but she disappears and it's just the hard slaps on my cheek, and
soon she is replaced with an image of my father. He's wearing a
green bomber jacket. There's snow all around us. He's holding me
by the neck, walking me back into the house. The social worker
called from school. I've been sick from sleeping outside. The cold
has gotten into my bones and I sit in my eighth-grade class shiver-
ing through the day. I'm always cold. The first slap comes over by
the fireplace. My sister is upstairs sleeping. My mother is dead four
months now. We're right by the couch she spent the last years of
her life on, virtually paralyzed and left alone most of the day with
her small black-and-white TV. I miss her so much and I don't
even know it yet. I haven't even begun to really think about her.
She died and I left, but now the social worker has called and my
father is angry so he tracked me down. I've been telling lies about
the family. I've betrayed him. I've made him look bad, done him
wrong. This is what is coming to me. This is what I have brought
on myself.

Eden is hitting me so hard while cradling my head in her hand.
The animal I sound like doesn't exist yet. Like a strange beast dying in the forest. My father's pulling me to the kitchen. There's
clippers there. He's shaving my head. I'm paralyzed with fear. Her
ropes are biting into me and I can't move. I see only him now.
Just my father, with no background, his green bomber jacket. Why
didn't I fight back? Because I've always been a coward.

And then he's replaced with another image, a year later. The state has taken custody. I was found with my wrists cut open, sleeping in an entryway. They asked me where my parents were; I told them I didn't know. They moved. I'm in a group home, just turned fifteen. There's a house meeting in the living room. I'm standing, holding a butter knife. The biggest boy in the home hits me open-handed across the face. "What are you going to do now?" he says. We're all wards of the court. We have nothing to lose. We shuttle from homes to institutions, between mental hospitals and jails. The staff stays seated, watching to see how this plays out. I could use some help.

I'm crying so hard and I can't stop. These are not the tears of love.

"Look at me," I hear. My eyes have been closed. Her face is there. Still kind. I don't even know what's happening. "Keep your eyes open." Her hand is still on my cheek. I can't seem to keep my eyes open. When I do, I keep crying. I want to scream and keep screaming. I want to say No! I try to close my eyes, to find my own head.

"Look at me."

What happened? I ask myself, but I know perfectly well what happened to me. I keep waiting for it to not have happened. Eden keeps saying she wants to give a space to that little boy inside me. Last time I spoke with my father, he said that was eighteen years ago already. It's time you get over it. I don't get over anything. I'm staring at Eden and I'm cracked into a million pieces. I want to do something for her. I don't even know what I could do.

I cry for so long. She has a gas mask in her bag. "I want to put this on you," she says. I push my face up toward it. I have rope burn between my legs. "I'm not going to put this on you yet, but I will soon." So I cry for a while longer but eventually I stop, and then the mask comes on. I can't tell when she's holding the mask closed except when I exhale and can't breathe back in. She keeps doing this until I'm panicking. We've been going for hours now. She holds her breath with me. She knows I should be able to hold my breath longer.

We don't know that her husband has been leaving messages on my phone. Her mother is OK. Her mother doesn't have cancer. It's just scar tissue. The phone is turned off. I can't breathe and I'm shaking my head, no no no no. And she's saying, "Are you saying no to me?" and I'm saying no, I'm not saying no to you. So I lie still and take what she wants to give me, which is what I always do when I think she's going too far: stretch myself out, take more, just to hear her say "Good boy." It's the only thing in the world worth hearing.

And when she's done she finally unties me, and I am stiff and sore and we lie in bed together. "It makes me wet to hit you," she says, and I slide my hand inside her pants to feel where her panties are damp. I rub her there. "I was so far gone," I say. "I was totally gone."

"You were, you were gone."

"Nobody's ever been as nice to me as you," I say.

"You haven't been hanging out with the right people."

Since meeting her I've wondered what it would have been like if I had met her earlier. Would I have been ready to accept what she offers? Would I still have been raped in a hotel room; done coke off a table while a man dressed in a nurse's outfit went down on three homeless men near Lake Michigan. Would I have accomplished anything; would I have needed to?

Eventually we go to dinner, but first we check my phone and find that her husband has called, and her mom, and the boy she owns, whom she takes to the clubs while he carries her things.

They've all called. How strange, I think, to be part of this family. They're all calling with the good news.

"I could cry," Eden says, but she doesn't.

At the restaurant we hold hands. This is one of our resolutions, to go out more. I suggest calling some friends, but neither of us wants to. Instead we go back to my apartment.

"I'm just setting you up," Eden says. "I'm going to leave you."

She's teasing.

"You're stepping on my emotional wires," I tell her.

We're not done. She lays a towel on my bed. "On your back," she says. I wonder if we need to do this. How are we connecting? Through our bodies, psychological closets we weren't supposed to open. But I don't care because I'll go wherever she wants to go.

I've given her the top drawer of my dresser and she keeps an extra shirt in there, a box of latex gloves, my collar, a large bottle of lube, rubbers, dental dams, a bracelet I made her from amber. I don't cry when she pushes her finger into my ass. I've written love stories before but they've never been happy. I wrote a whole book about the urge to substitute abuse for affection. The last girl I dated had me call her Daddy, hit me from anger when we were walking down the street, kicked me out of her apartment in the middle of the night, and I walked home from there and witnessed a car crash while standing beneath the overhang of a convenience store wondering what I should do.

"When you write," Eden says. "You make yourself sound damaged and you insist that you're a coward. But you're not. You're strong." Maybe if she keeps telling me that, I'll believe it, but I'm not ready for that yet.

Even with all the lube, it hurts, her hand in my ass. And then I fall asleep. I go. I have nothing left. I dream for moments and then forget my dreams, awakening to the sharp pain of her withdrawal. "Talk to me for a while," she says. "How did it feel?"

"It felt good," I say. But I'm always afraid when she does that. "I felt you go to sleep," she says. "I felt your body loosen up."

I try to talk to her more but I can't. In the morning my flight is so early and I'll be gone for so long. Twelve days. It seems forever, but I'm almost feeling like I can make it, and I know it'll only take me a day to change my mind about that. But there are no options. Even if I stayed she'd have to spend the next two days with her son and husband and then on Sunday she leaves for a week. I could stay but I can't make her stay.

"Touch me," she says. It's six in the morning. The sun is lighting my curtains. I slide my fingers between her legs. "I smell like garlic down there. From the meatloaf last night."

"You have garlic cooch," I say. She hasn't shaved her legs, her armpits. I think of Frank Zappa singing "Give me your dirty love." This is not something I would have done—joked about body fluids, made love in the morning before brushing my teeth—but this is what I do now. I don't care anything about who I was before. That person is gone.

She drives me to the airport. The highways are clear across the bay, and I stroke her leg while crossing the bridge. We're early, so we sit in the short-term parking lot. "Imagine a lake in front of us," I say. "We're on a cliff, surrounded by trees. The sky is like velvet, covered in stars." She reaches across my waist, slides my chair back, climbs into my lap.

When it's time she walks me to the gate. "This is so romantic," I say. "You took me to the airport. You're walking me to the terminal. It's like going steady."

"Does that mean I get a ring?" she asks.

She has rings. She has a wedding ring, an engagement ring. Last night in the restaurant we were talking about the war, and I told her I was a British citizen and that when it came to it we'd move somewhere in the Commonwealth, keep her safe. I wasn't talking about her husband, but she thought I was. "We'd have to get married for that to be true," she said. I wanted to tell her I was only joking, but I didn't. I said, "I could marry you." And what I meant was that maybe, if we were together five years from now, we could have a ceremony, or something. It didn't matter. "I don't believe in divorce," she said, sticking her fork into her food. "For me I don't believe in it, I mean."

Inside the terminal, we're running out of time. We kiss, and then we kiss some more.

"You made me cry, feeding me chocolate," I say. "You were so pretty."

There is nothing left except platitudes, all of them true. I love you. I'll miss you. I'll think about you every day. I'll call. I'll e-mail. I'll see you again.

I feel clear, stepping through the checkpoint. The plane is already boarding. The truth is that everything is fine. Even Eden's husband has grown comfortable with the situation. He's agreed that Eden can sleep over at my house once a week starting when I get back. The future is bright. This is a happy story.

Out There:
Mountain as a New Bridge
Jeff Weinstein

I've seen *Brokeback Mountain* twice now, and each time have left the theater unutterably, helplessly sad. I cannot deny the power of true and passionate art to move us, and moved I was, even more after the second try. Yet I wondered about and even mistrusted the gray helplessness that for days I couldn't shake.

Some of us have spent years fighting the miserable fate that this heartbreaking film awards to its two thwarted men in love. Is it worth being dragged back, if only through the movie screen and my easily led imagination, to such a dangerous place? For gay and nongay viewers both, I'm surprised to find that the answer is yes.

My reasoning has come not through obvious logic, but in pieces.

Like so many others whose real lives never fully emerge in the give-and-take of popular culture, I grew up ravenous to read any book or see any movie in which something, anything, gay managed to peek through. At first it made no difference whether the fiction was lurid—as in John Rechy's *City of Night*—or the films nasty and belittling. We pre-Stonewallers pored over these secret treats as if they were Rosetta Stones that someday we'd be able to decipher.

And so I became more than a little impatient when I finally realized that it was up to the culture to decipher me.

Here's one memory, from 1982:

I was sitting in a theater next to Vito Russo, an ebullient activist and author of *The Celluloid Closet,* a groundbreaking book about gay film history. We were there because a new movie, *Making Love,* starring Harry Hamlin, Michael Ontkean, and Charlie's Angel Kate Jackson, was oh-so-quietly touted as the first big Hollywood film about a gay relationship.

Too bad that dead direction resulted in a tepid movie, not nearly as rich or risky as John Schlesinger's 1971 *Sunday Bloody Sunday,* an art-house gem about a three-way relationship starring the glorious Glenda Jackson and masterful Peter Finch. Yet, when Michael's and Harry's lips first touched, in close-up, on that wide, wide screen, Vito and I turned to each other and even in the darkness could see our eyes moisten up.

Nothing needed to be said. Although we expected that some people in most audiences would laugh and retch and more or less run screaming toward the door (which is exactly what happened) when faced with the indisputable cinematic evidence that two men could love, a bridge had been crossed and nothing would be the same.

Vito Russo died of AIDS eight years later, and, for good or for bad, that calamitous disease became popular culture's primary gay vehicle, leavened by the occasional feisty drag queen or limp best buddy. Perhaps you remember Tom Hanks in the kissless AIDS classic named after the City of Brotherly Love.

Now, almost awash in a televised queer materialism that is anxious to say our gay troubles are over, we have another *Making Love*—with no Vito to turn to. The "bridge" itself, though much better built, is sadly very much the same. But this time, will the great mass audience, my neighbors and colleagues, my readers and friends, stay in their seats and cross it?

I don't want to be a spoiler for you who are planning to go see it, but I can attempt to say why *Brokeback Mountain,* set in rural Wyoming from the 1960s to the '80s, is so shattering.

The story, by Wyoming resident Annie Proulx, on which the faithful screenplay is based was written a short time before the young gay man Matthew Shepard was beaten and murdered outside Laramie, with a vista of Brokebacks as background. Don't get your spurs tangled in the cheap joke that this is a movie about "gay cowboys." Its main characters are—as the author herself has said—merely two dirt-poor and unconnected young men who...

Who are written into a story in which they, because of their class, upbringing, and inescapable values, values they live and breathe, seem to have no choice but to come to desolate conclusions. One man is trapped by fear, by the utter absence of personal possibility. And so the other man, who has hints of how their love could live, is trapped as well.

Theirs is an American tragedy of the old school, put in motion by the same fictional fatalism that says gingham girlfriend Shelley Winters must be taken out in a rowboat to the middle of a lake and drowned, and starry-eyed climber Montgomery Clift, looking for his place in the sun, must be the one to push her.

In spite of its nervous packaging and self-serving studio quotes, *Brokeback* isn't a universal *Romeo and Juliet,* a tale of love hampered that anyone can enjoy. It's a story of *gay* love hampered, gay love destroyed—enjoy it if you can.

An unrelated memory:

When I first visited Laramie sometime in the mid-1970s, a gay and lesbian group had just formed at the city's university. Would I go on campus radio and talk about gay life, a cordial professor asked? Of course, I said—and the next day the request was withdrawn, no explanation. My Laramie hosts also warned me not to walk the trim and pleasant streets of the town alone.

Just before World War I, English author E. M. Forster wrote a novel called *Maurice*—the too-lush movie was made in 1987—about two quite different men from quite different classes who fall thoroughly in love. The book wasn't published until the author died decades later; he was afraid, he had said, of offending his mother.

The English cards were stacked, no doubt, against this pair too, but Forster, to his eternal credit, gives them a fantasy out, an escape to an arcadian world where they and their like may do as their hearts demand. Forster found a fictional hope.

Odd fact is that the fussy author managed to live happily with his working-class policeman lover for quite a long time, no arcadia needed.

I can't tell you that *Brokeback Mountain* is a great film, great in the *Citizen Kane* sense. What I can say is what makes it unique—a word all writers fear to use—and exquisitely touching.

There's a scene early on, as the two men are getting to know each other during their first summer on Brokeback, when Ennis (Heath Ledger) strips and washes himself from a basin. Jack (Jake Gyllenhaal), in the foreground, out of some combination of decency, embarrassment, and sweet care, doesn't turn around to steal a glance.

The absence of familiar workaday lust, and then the overwhelming rush of sexual passion and riveting, wrenching, inconceivable love is absolutely new.

I have waited in the dark for that cultural verification all of my life.

About the Authors

DAVID AMSDEN is the author of the novel *Important Things That Don't Matter*. His fiction and nonfiction appear regularly in *Details*, *Slate*, *Salon*, the *Believer*, and *New York* magazine, where he is a contributing editor. He lives in Brooklyn, and is currently working on a personal and reportorial account of kids in their teens and early twenties.

SHALOM AUSLANDER is the author of *Beware of God: Stories* and has been a frequent contributor to *Esquire* magazine and NPR's *This American Life*.

SUSANNAH BRESLIN is the author of *You're a Bad Man, Aren't You?*, a short story collection from Future Tense Books. Her nonfiction, fiction, photographs, and comics have appeared in *Details*, *Harper's Bazaar*, *LA Weekly*, Nerve.com, *Variety*, and many other publications. Currently, she is at work on a book about Porn Valley. Her website can be found at www.invisiblecowgirl.com.

SUSIE BRIGHT is editor of *The Best American Erotica* series, author of *Susie Sexpert's Lesbian Sex World*, *Susie Bright's Sexual Reality*, *Sexwise*, and many other books on erotica and sexual politics. She is the radio host of *In Bed With Susie Bright*, on Audible.com, and can be found at http://susiebright.com.

EMILY DePRANG is a writer living in New York. Her work has appeared in *FHM* and at Nerve.com, among other places. She is currently writing *If, Then*, a memoir of her marriage to a female-to-male transsexual.

STEPHEN ELLIOTT is the author of five books, including *Happy Baby*, a finalist for the New York Public Library's Young Lion Award as well as a best book of 2004 in Salon.com, *Newsweek*, *New City Chicago*, and the *Village Voice*. He is a contributing writer for the *Believer*, the *San Francisco Chronicle*, *Newsday*, the *Village Voice*, and *McSweeney's*, and his work has been featured in *Esquire*, the *New York Times*, *GQ*, *Best American Non-Required Reading*, and *Best American Erotica*. Stephen Elliott's collection *My Girlfriend Comes to the City and Beats Me Up* is forthcoming from Cleis Press in fall 2006. He lives in San Francisco. Visit him online at www.stephenelliott.com.

PAUL FESTA's essays and criticism have appeared in *Salon*, *Nerve*, *Best Sex Writing 2005*, and other publications. His experimental documentary *Apparition of the Eternal Church* premiered at the 2005 Asheville Film Festival. Currently revising a novel, he lives in San Francisco and can be found on the Web at www.paulfesta.com.

John Cameron Mitchell's "Sex Film Project," now called "Shortbus," is, at press time (April 2006), in post-production.

MICHAEL A. GONZALES has written articles for *Essence*, the *Village Voice*, *Spin*, Popmatters.com, *XXL*, and *Entertainment Weekly*. A former writer-at-large for *Vibe*, he has contributed short fiction to *Bronx Biannual*, *Uptown*, *Trace*, and the first three volumes of the *Brown Sugar* erotica series. He lives in Brooklyn.

NATALIE Y. MOORE is a freelance journalist and part-time college instructor in Chicago. NATALIE HOPKINSON is a *Washington Post* staff writer and a Scripps Howard Doctoral Fellow in media studies at the University of Maryland–College Park. Their book, *Deconstructing Tyrone: A New Look at Black Masculinity in the Hip-Hop Generation*, is forthcoming from Cleis Press in fall 2006.

ALEX MORRIS is a writer in New York City.

ANNALEE NEWITZ is a San Francisco–based writer whose work focuses on the intersection of culture, science, and technology. She's a contributing editor at *Wired*, editor of *other* magazine, and writes the syndicated weekly column "Techsploitation." Find out more at www.techsploitation.com.

MICHELLE ORANGE has written for *McSweeney's*, Salon.com, the *Sun*, the *San Francisco Chronicle*, *Brick* magazine, and other publications. Her most recent work, *The Sicily Papers*, is available from Hobart Pulp. She lives in New York City.

MARK PRITCHARD is the author of two collections of erotic stories, *Too Beautiful and Other Stories* and *How I Adore You*, published by Cleis Press in 2001, and is the former coeditor/publisher of *Frighten the Horses*. His website is at www.toobeautiful.org.

ELI SANDERS is a staff writer for the *Stranger*, an alternative weekly in Seattle. His work has appeared in the *New York Times*, the *Boston Globe*, the *Seattle Times*, and *Time* magazine.

TRISTAN TAORMINO is the author of *True Lust: Adventures in Sex, Porn and Perversion*; *Down and Dirty Sex Secrets*; and *The Ultimate Guide to Anal Sex for Women*. She is a columnist for the *Village Voice* and *Taboo* and is editrix of her site, Puckerup.com.

VIRGINIA VITZTHUM is a former sex columnist for Salon.com and has also written for the *Village Voice*, the *Washington Post*, *Elle*, *Ms.*, and other publications. Her book about online dating is forthcoming from Little, Brown in spring 2007. She lives in Brooklyn.

JEFF WEINSTEIN, a culture editor at Bloomberg News, has been fine arts editor and popular culture columnist at the *Philadelphia Inquirer* and a columnist and senior editor at the *Village Voice*. Author of *Life in San Diego* and *Learning To Eat*, both published by Sun & Moon Press, he has written for the *New Yorker*, *Artforum*, *Art in America*, the *Advocate*, and many other publications.

About the Editors

FELICE NEWMAN and FREDERIQUE DELACOSTE are the founding publishers of Cleis Press. Frédérique Delacoste is the editor of *Sex Work: Writings by Women in the Sex Industry*. She lives in London and San Francisco. Felice Newman is the author of *The Whole Lesbian Sex Book: A Passionate Guide for All of Us*. She is a certified somatic coach, and writes on sexuality in print and online. She lives in the San Francisco Bay Area. Visit her at www.felicenewman.com.